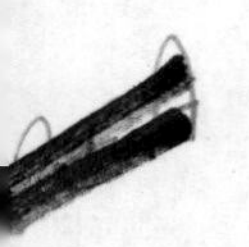

Returning Home for Easter
The Lenten Journey

Returning Home for Easter
The Lenten Journey

Richard Gribble, CSC

Library of Congress Cataloging-in-Publication Data

Gribble, Richard.
Returning home for Easter : the Lenten journey / Richard Gribble.
p. cm.
ISBN 0-8198-6465-X
1. Lent—Prayer-books and devotions—English. I. Title.
BX2170.L4G735 1997
242'.34—dc20 96-29361
CIP

http://www.pauline.org

E-mail: PBM_EDIT@INTERRAMP.COM

Printed and published in the U.S.A. by Pauline Books & Media, 50 St. Paul's Avenue, Boston, MA 02130.

Pauline Books & Media is the publishing house of the Daughters of St. Paul, an international congregation of women religious serving the Church with the communications media.

1 2 3 4 99 98 97

Dedication

This book was written through the inspiration of daily prayer and the gifts God has given me for reflection and writing. My life has been blessed with many sources of inspiration: family, good friends and the support of my religious community. However, this particular book finds its source of inspiration in a comment of my friend Mary, "My reason for life is to return to God." Her spirit touches my heart and speaks of God's love for me. For Mary, therefore, this book is written.

Table of Contents

Introduction

Steven Spielberg's 1982 motion picture classic, *E.T.—The Extra Terrestrial,* captured the hearts and minds of moviegoers around the world with its combination of comedy, drama and tragedy. The plot of the film described E.T.'s quest to "go home" and was framed in the context of the relationship between the visitor from space and his human friend Elliot. E.T., who was left behind accidentally when his spaceship was forced to flee from human intrusion, is lost in a world which cannot understand or accept his presence. E.T. knows he will die if he remains in the earth's environment, so he must return home. At the end of the movie, when his friends return to earth to retrieve him, he feels a sense of triumph that he has met the challenge and can now return home, to a place which will welcome him and where he can grow to new heights.

E.T.'s trial on earth and his need and desire to go home parallels in many ways the annual opportunity which all Christians can experience during the season of Lent. In her wisdom the Church provides this period of preparation so that we can search our hearts for ways to better prepare ourselves for our ultimate return to the God who made us and fashioned us in his image. Our preparation during the Lenten season is immediately oriented toward the Easter Triduum when we celebrate the passion, death and resurrection of the Lord. But a broader view shows that this season is a gift which brings special opportunities in our daily life to prepare for our return home to God. Sometimes, like E.T., our communication link with our heavenly home is cut or functions poorly, through lack of use or other problems. Lent is a time to retune our communication system so that we can, as the song from the popular musical *Godspell* says, "see thee more clearly, love thee more dearly, follow thee more nearly, day by day."

This book is a series of meditations based on the daily and Sunday readings for Mass in the Lenten season. Although the meditations were written to stand alone as thoughts that can aid our search for God, they can be more helpful when used together with the readings upon which they are based. The reader is encouraged to use this book in conjunction with reading Scripture in a daily walk with the Lord. It is my hope that your preparation during this season of grace will aid your journey home to God, that you will find renewal of spirit, and in the end, make your hearts ready to receive the resurrected Lord.

Richard Gribble, CSC

Meditations for the Week of Ash Wednesday

Ash Wednesday

Readings: Joel 2:12-18;
2 Corinthians 5:20-6:2; Matthew 6:1-6, 16-18

Going Home

At times we all yearn to go home. Going home may mean returning to the place of our birth or the house where we grew up, or it may mean our homecoming after a vacation, business trip or time at college. But going home does not happen without laying some groundwork. For some people it might only require a phone call informing those at home that they are on the way. Others might have to plan a trip, considering time, money and method if a long distance is involved. Sometimes we may dread going home because of previous events, strained relationships or unanswered questions. If we return home it is necessary to wait and make arrangements; we must prepare ourselves, each person in a different way.

Ultimately the sole reason that God created us and the only vital goal in our lives must be to return home to God. Along the road, God showers us with multiple and varied gifts and asks us to contribute to building the kingdom in our world. We participate in this effort individually and collectively by leading lives of discipleship and holiness, placing ourselves at the service of others, especially the lowly and those unable to repay our efforts. God has much for us to do, but all our labors lead us toward the final goal of union with the Creator, the source of all life and goodness.

Lent, our annual season of grace which gives us the opportunity to prepare ourselves to return home, begins today by asking us to look into our hearts to determine what we need most in getting ready for our homecoming with the Lord. The prophet Joel tells us, "Rend your hearts and not your clothing. Return to the Lord, your God, for he is gracious and merciful" (Joel 2:13). He proclaims that the trumpet must be blown and the people gathered; they are to awake and begin the inner journey of self-reflection. Preparation for our journey home must begin with an evaluation of the heart. Some of what we discover on the inward search will please us because it comes from God, but other things will disappoint us, especially when we realize that our own lack of effort, refusal to listen or inability to love has cast darkness on our souls. Our self-discovery may require us to mend a fence or two along the road.

Fortunately, through such an inner journey we come to know our need to be reconciled, to self, one another, and finally to God. Paul tells the Corinthians, "Be reconciled to God!" (2 Cor 5:20). Jesus Christ, the Word incarnate, understands our human frailty and knows our need for reconciliation. The Lord undertook the journey of introspection many times—a night in prayer to the Father, the temptation at the hand of Satan, and the agony in the Garden of Gethsemane—all in preparation to return to God who sent him. Jesus' experience in his own private Lent, his preparation for Calvary, must be our example as we make this special journey during this season of grace.

Once we look inside, discover and accept ourselves, and then find reconciliation, we are ready for the discipline which Lent asks of us. Traditionally, as Jesus suggests in Matthew's Gospel, the Church finds its discipline in the areas of almsgiving, fasting and prayer. True charity asks us to give from the heart and not just the mind. To be an almsgiver necessitates our dedication but it also requires our reflection on why we do what we do—for self or for the Lord? Fasting and prayer can be conducted in public ways, but again, who are we trying to impress? As Matthew says, God sees into the heart, which is all that matters.

The journey of Lent has begun and so too our preparation for going home. Whether God calls us tonight or in seventy years, we must prepare for it with sincere hearts. As this special season begins, let us look into our hearts, seek reconciliation with self, others and God, and then begin to discipline ourselves for this journey to death, resurrection, and in the end, eternal life.

Thursday after Ash Wednesday

Readings: Deuteronomy 30:15-20; Luke 9:22-25

Death Leads to Life

"When Christ calls a man, he calls him to come and die." The famous Lutheran pastor and theologian, Dietrich Bonhoeffer, wrote those words in his influential book, *The Cost of Discipleship*. Bonhoeffer lived his Christian call to holiness without counting the cost; he never looked back or questioned what God asked of him. Bonhoeffer lived as he wrote—he knew that a life of true discipleship would cost him everything. Born in Prussia in 1906, Bonhoeffer was raised in Berlin where his father was a professor of neurology and psychiatry. Gifted intellectually, he studied theology and earned a doctorate writing on Swiss theologian Karl Barth's contemporary concept of the "theology of revelation."

Bonhoeffer served as a pastor, and became a popular speaker and well-known writer. He never wavered from his Christian commitment, even after 1933 brought the rise of Adolph Hitler and his Nazi ideology of godlessness and anti-Semitism. Bonhoeffer strongly opposed Hitler and continued for five years to operate an underground seminary for Germany's "Confessing Church," the leading German Protestant resistance movement, although it was proscribed in 1937. Eventually the Nazis caught up with him and imprisoned him in April 1943. While in prison he wrote his most significant and popular work, *Prisoner of God: Letters and Papers from Prison.*

Implicated in the failed July 1944 plot to assassinate Hitler, Bonhoeffer was sent to a concentration camp in Flössenberg, Bavaria, where the Nazis executed him on April 9, 1945. Dietrich Bonhoeffer died as he lived, promoting the Christian truths which had become his life; he was a martyr who chose death so that others might live.

Dietrich Bonhoeffer's story exemplifies what our readings today convey to us—we can find life only through death. Any rational-thinking person seeks life, which is the most basic drive that we possess. Moses certainly knew this and so when he spoke to the Hebrews he enjoined them, "Choose life so that you and your descendants may live, loving the Lord your God, obeying him, and holding fast to him" (Dt 30:19-20). But what is the life which Moses asks the people to seek? Is it a life for self or for God? Certainly the answer is a life for God. Life for self is finite and can realize only a fraction of our potentiality, but life for God, lived for and through God's people, has no limits and possesses all possibilities. This was the goal for the people of Israel; it must be ours as well.

Jesus gave the best example in his teaching and life of what it means to live for others. In today's Gospel the Lord proposes the classic Christian paradox: "For those who want to save their life will lose it, and those who lose their life for my sake will save it" (Lk 9:24). On the surface Jesus' comment appears nonsensical, but like all paradoxes it is actually true. God asks us to die to self and sacrifice our own needs for those of others. Society may not highly prize such a value, especially with our contemporary "all for me" mentality, but the Christian life has always been radical in its demands, beginning with Jesus who daily challenged society and his disciples to seek higher things.

The road home to the Lord leads to our death; yet we all shrink from death with every ounce of our strength. The courageous path on the road home is to live for others. God seldom calls a person to act with the fervor of Dietrich Bonhoeffer, but it is through such examples and those of other contemporary martyrs, like Oscar Romero and Maximilian Kolbe, that we might summon the courage to die to self so others may live more fully. Let us today reflect on our need to follow Christ more fully—to death and eternal life.

Friday after Ash Wednesday

Readings: Isaiah 58:1-9; Matthew 9:14-15

Feeding Others

An ancient Asian tale speaks of two images which contrast the difference between heaven and hell. The image of hell is this: There is a large banquet hall adorned with all the finest that money can buy. The table and chairs are made of oak from the Black Forest of Germany; the linen is handmade by European craftsmen. The table is set with Waterford crystal and plates and saucers made of bone china. The meal itself has been prepared by the world's best chefs. All the guests are dressed in their finest attire. The only odd thing about this scene is that the silverware utensils, made of sterling silver, are long, heavy and cumbersome. When the guests sit down and begin to eat some people can't lift any of the utensils. Those that can lift a fork, knife or spoon cannot maneuver it so as to get anything to eat. Soon banqueters begin to bump into each other. Frustration mounts and tempers flare. In the end no one gets anything to eat.

The image of heaven is a bit different. The same banquet hall is adorned in the same way. The Black Forest oak, linen, bone china, Waterford crystal, and fine food are all present, along with the large and cumbersome silverware. Dressed very smartly, a different group of guests mill around. Somehow these banqueters have learned an important lesson. They realize that the utensils will not allow them to feed themselves. Thus, when they sit down to eat, those who can lift the utensils pick up food and maneuver it so as to feed a neighbor. When necessary two people lift a fork and feed a third person, who, in turn, feeds those who fed him. In the end all eat well; each person is satisfied, because everyone has learned to feed each other.

These contrasting images tell us something very important about the concept of fasting described in today's readings. Most people instinctively think of fasting in negative terms, an action of giving up or self-denial. But in the words of Isaiah the prophet, God says that the best type of fast is one in which we feed others. In this third section of his book, Isaiah writes to the Hebrew people who have returned from exile in Babylon. They have had fifty years to reflect upon their relationship with God, to ponder God's message and the covenant. During this time they had suffered and had been deprived of many things that they had taken for granted in their native land. But God wants them to know that their experience was not without purpose; they have learned a valuable lesson about transforming adversity into a blessing. Fasting as self-denial can be turned into an action where others are fed not only with food but, more importantly, with human support. Isaiah speaks powerfully: "Is not this the fast that I choose: to loose the bonds of injustice, to undo the thongs of the yoke, to let the oppressed go free, and to break every yoke? Is it not to share your bread with the hungry, and bring the homeless poor into your house; when you see the naked, to cover them, and not to hide yourself from your own kin?" (Is 58:6-7).

The Book of Ecclesiastes (3:1-8) suggests that there is a time and season for all things, and so it is with fasting.

Jesus knows that a time will come when his apostles will suffer much, fast, and feed others, but not when he is with them. So too for us there is a time for personal celebration and a time to think more of others. Lent is the time to right our own spiritual ship. Then we can feed others by what we do and say so that they, as the Asian tale suggests, may in turn nourish us.

On this first Friday of Lent we know that the Church asks us to refrain from meat in our meals as a sign that we remember the great events that occurred on the Friday Jesus died for us. As we live this day of abstinence, let us think of ways that we can feed others, transform self-denial into positive practice, and imitate Jesus, our brother, friend and Lord.

Saturday after Ash Wednesday

Readings: Isaiah 58:9-14; Luke 5:27-32

Negotiating the Maze of Life

Puzzles, especially those that require one to go from point A to point B, pose a great challenge for those who attempt to solve them. If a mouse or hamster is placed in a maze, one can observe the difficulties and frustrations it experiences in its quest to find the finish line and a way out. The animal will bump into walls, take wrong turns, find itself backed into a corner or even return to the start. The one thing that seems to help is experience. If an animal has been challenged in the past to run a maze, then it has a greater chance to succeed. No signs or directions show the correct way; experience and a certain amount of fortune are necessary to find the solution to the maze.

Humans must negotiate many tortuous courses over the span of our life. We can sharpen our skills for solving puzzles by actually working to complete them. More importantly, however, we are constantly challenged to figure out the many mazes of life which we find in work, family, community and religion. As the expression goes, life is a great teacher with the many experiences which come our way. Often the new course in life which we are asked to walk has no directions or signs; we sometimes operate blindly, with only faith and hope that things will come out right and we will be where we should.

Life throws us many curves which challenge us and lead to frustration. When faced with an uncertain path and no directions, we have the natural tendency to shy away from the journey. We wish to stay where we are, with our present knowledge and its relative certainty, rather than venture into new waters. Yet growth requires us to move beyond where we are now and take the risk of getting lost along the way. We should have confidence, however, that if we summon the strength to meet the challenge we have a guide who will lead us home. Isaiah tells us in today's reading that the Lord will guide us always, provide light in the darkness, renew our strength, and sustain us like a spring whose water never fails. The Hebrew people to whom Isaiah wrote had just experienced God's guiding hand in their return to Israel after the exile, so they knew well the truth of the prophet's words.

Jesus is our constant guide and companion as we negotiate the various hurdles, obstacles and mazes of life. As humans we are incomplete, broken and in need of God's presence. Jesus certainly knew this reality. In the Gospel he speaks of how he came to lead home those who seek a change of heart in their lives. Jesus is the great healer, the physician who cures our spiritual ills so that we can more completely experience the fullness of life.

On the way home we need to make periodic checks on our spiritual lives. Our return to God is filled with many obstacles, some of which we control by our own actions and others over which we have absolutely no control. If we look inside at our lives and seriously review and accept who we are, then we can begin again to follow the signs Jesus provides to lead us home. The Lord's call of Matthew the tax collector, a notorious sinner in the eyes of the Jewish people, shows that Jesus is present and willing to assist and guide all who call upon him in sincerity and truth. Jesus cannot keep us from the frustrations, bumps and bruises of this life, for we live in an imperfect and sinful world. But the Master can lead us home by guiding us through the maze of life. Our task greatly challenges us, but with faith and perseverance we will get where we need and want to be. Let us overcome the hurdles of this life by following the lead of the great physician, Jesus, and thereby unravel the maze that leads to eternal life.

Meditations for the First Week of Lent

Sunday Week I (Year A)

Readings: Genesis 2:7-9; 3:1-7, Romans 5:12-19; Matthew 4:1-11

Loyalty to God or the World

He was a man of mystery and charm; he was a man of brokenness and faith. Hunted down like a common criminal, his only crime was seeking God's glory. The "Whiskey Priest" lived in Southern Mexico in the 1920s during the Cristero Rebellion. He was not perfect—far from it. He drank too much and he fathered a child. In those days the government said that it was illegal to practice the priesthood, but that did not stop the Whiskey Priest. Everything that he did, the Masses, baptisms and funerals, had to be conducted in secret.

The *federales* (a band of soldiers) and their commanding lieutenant represented the power of the government. Their job was to find the Whiskey Priest, to stop his activity and ultimately, to eliminate him. The hunt went from town to town, village to village. In one village where the lieutenant knew the Whiskey Priest had been, the residents would say nothing. The lieutenant's methods became more persuasive; he shot five villagers to loosen their tongues.

The Whiskey Priest knew that he was living on borrowed time. He continued to move from town to town. The winter rains helped him "disappear" in the mountain highlands. The *federales* would win; it was just a matter of time. In the end he was found and executed, a common criminal to the government, a martyr to the people.

Graham Greene's epic story *The Power and the Glory* contrasts imperfect humanity struggling for the glory of God with a society seeking power and destruction. On this First Sunday of Lent our readings describe the same challenging option. The Book of Genesis describes how the desire for power was born into the human race. Adam and Eve had all that they needed since God had totally provided for them. Still, they wanted more. They wanted all knowledge; they wanted to become like God. Their desire for power cost them everything. With the knowledge they gained, they lost their innocence. Their desire to be like God only produced problems. Adam and Eve caved into the outside pressure. Temptation had won. Power triumphed and sin entered the world.

In the Gospel we hear the famous story of Jesus' temptation in the desert. The Lord serves as a contrast to Adam. Jesus is offered the three treasures of our world, but he never gives in to the temptation. The first temptation is to grasp power, seen in the offer of changing stones into bread. Jesus does not need power—concentrating on God's word is more important. Prestige is the second great temptation, seen in the challenge to throw himself from the temple. Satan chides Jesus, saying that he is an important person and thus his angels will care for him. Christ responds by saying that he does not need to show such prestige. The fact that Jesus is God is prestige enough. The final temptation is to wealth, as Satan offers to grant all the kingdoms of the world to Jesus. "Bow down and worship me," Satan challenges. Jesus responds that he does not need such riches. Jesus will not honor Satan, for only God is to be worshipped.

In writing to the Christian community at Rome, St. Paul summarizes all that we have heard. The Apostle says that through one man, Adam, sin entered the world—original sin, a condition that afflicts all people. It is the reality that we live in a world which can be filled with joy, but is also plagued with problems and pain. But through Jesus the sin of the world is remitted and we are all acquitted. Through the presence of Jesus we can live in this sometimes cruel world and flourish.

As we celebrate this first Sunday in Lent we must ask ourselves where we stand, with God or the world? Concerning power, does the desire for power consume us? If we have power, do we use it for personal gain or for the betterment of all? Is power a thing of value and a necessity, or can we live without it? With regard to prestige, do we do things so others will notice? Do we use our position to dominate others? Or do we seek the glory of God and not concern ourselves with what society might think? With respect to wealth, are we seeking to surpass our neighbor by what we have? Does our world revolve around money? Is it the solution to all our problems? In short, have power, prestige and money become the gods to which we pay homage?

Today as our Lenten journey begins in earnest, let us evaluate our approach to life. Am I the imperfect human, the Whiskey Priest of society, who moves toward the Lord and seeks God's glory? Or am I a *federale* who seeks the power of the world? God challenges us today to seek the higher realms. How will we respond?

Sunday Week I (Year B)

Readings: Genesis 9:8-15;
1 Peter 3:18-22; Mark 1:12-15

The Trials of Life

Carlo Rienzi, an attorney with no mission or case, had never come to trial. He was fearful and apprehensive, because he had never been tested. He did not want the trial that he knew must come. When the case came it seemed impossible. A young woman had shot the mayor of a small village without provocation—at least so it seemed on the surface. The court assigned Carlo as the woman's legal defense. Everything seemed to be against him; the evidence was overwhelming. The people in the town had loved their mayor and they could see no reason why he should have been killed. The whole town rallied against Carlo and his client. Although the woman faced the jury, the trial for Carlo may have been greater. It tested his character. Could he perform as he had been trained; would he hold up under the pressure? The trial tested his will as well. In the face of overwhelming adversity could he stay with his client and give her a fair and complete defense?

Although the evidence was against him Carlo's perseverance would win the day. The trial took place in a small courtroom in the village where the crime had been committed. Carlo went to the place of the trial in order to find himself. In his investigation Carlo Rienzi discovered a reason for the young woman's actions. He learned that the mayor was not the kind and gentle man which most people in the village thought they knew; he had a mysterious past. In the end Carlo's client was convicted, but she received the lightest sentence possible for the crime. As a lawyer Carlo Rienzi had been tried and found worthy.

Morris West's novel *Daughter of Silence* tells the story of the testing of a man and how he found himself through that experience. During Lent, we are tested and challenged to find ourselves and experience our faith in greater and fuller ways. In the Gospel Jesus goes to the desert to prepare for his mission in life. While there, Satan puts him to the test. The trial is a series of temptations to all the allurements of this world. Jesus survives the period of trial; he is found worthy and angels come to wait on him. Jesus is now ready to go forth and begin his mission. His message is clear, "Reform your lives; the reign of God is near."

God has tested the world as well. In the first reading we hear that people had sunk into evil and refused to listen to God. Therefore, the great flood was sent to purify the world. Yet some persons had remained faithful. Noah and his family lived in God's presence and they survived their period of trial. Because of the faithfulness of Noah, God made a covenant with humanity—never again would a great flood destroy the world.

In our daily lives God sets before us many challenges and situations which can try us greatly. Like Jesus, our trek to the desert, our Lenten journey, can be a great challenge, a desert experience. It can make us better and more complete people. In Morris West's novel Carlo Rienzi made himself something through meeting a challenge head on, by succeeding through his perseverance.

Similarly, Jesus became perfect through suffering his own personal trial, as the Letter to the Hebrews tells us (cf. Heb 2:10). Our lives are filled with trials. There are challenges at work with our business associates, with the boss, and with our duties. There are challenges at school, with classmates, teachers and homework assignments. There are challenges in life, with its problems, illness, suffering and death.

How do we handle all these trials? The answer is to go to the desert, like Carlo Rienzi and Jesus did, and we'll find the solution there. The solutions to life's trials are found in prayer, works of mercy and fasting, the traditional Lenten observances. None of these works change God. As we know, God is all knowing, all loving and immutable. But through prayer, works of mercy, and fasting *we* change. We can then accept the difficulties of life. More importantly, we can accept God's will in our lives. Through trial and challenge we grow and through prayer we learn acceptance.

Today the Lenten journey takes us to the desert to begin a time of trial and testing. Even though this test may be difficult we believe that it allows us to grow and accept the will of God in our lives. Today, therefore, let us seek the challenge of the desert and turn to prayer in our lives. Let us be transformed on our personal journey to Calvary and resurrection.

Sunday Week I (Year C)

Readings: Deuteronomy 26:4-10;
Romans 10:8-13; Luke 4:1-13

Place Your Trust in the Lord

A team of world famous botanists was exploring rugged terrain in the rain forests of Brazil searching for rare forms of plant life. The scientists, who came from all over the world, were excited about this particular mission with its opportunity to examine unexplored territory. As the team made its way through thick brush the members discovered some unknown ferns and fauna. One day the leader of the expedition was scanning a ravine with his binoculars. He spotted an exotic flower which he believed had never been catalogued. He called his colleagues and they all looked at this rare discovery from a distance. The flower was growing deep in the ravine with high cliffs rising on each side; the only way to get to it would be to lower someone over the side with a rope. The task bristled with danger.

A young lad happened along the scene quite unexpectedly. Curious about the scientists' work, the boy came over to talk with them. The head of the expedition told him, "We will give you fifty dollars if you will allow us to lower you over the side of this cliff so you can reach the beautiful flower." The boy surveyed the situation and looked deep into the ravine which housed the rare plant. "Wait one minute," the boy said, "I'll be right back." A few minutes later the young lad returned accompanied by an older man. "I will go over the side and get the flower for you," said the lad to the chief scientist, "as long as this man holds the rope. He is my father."

In a similar situation whom would you trust—a stranger or a friend? In general whom do we trust—members of our family, relatives, friends, neighbors, colleagues at work? Do we place our hope and trust in the things of this world or do we have the courage to place our trust in our heavenly Father, the source of all that is good? Our readings today challenge us to place our trust in the Lord who cares for us and will rescue us in time of need.

We know from reading the Hebrew Scriptures that God chose the Israelites to be a people peculiarly his own. They were a special people. God gave them the patriarchs, Abraham, Isaac and Jacob. God sent Moses to deliver the people from bondage in Egypt. Through Moses, God led them through the Red Sea, gave them the law, fed them with manna and, as we hear in today's reading, brought them to the threshold of the Promised Land, flowing with milk and honey. God has been ever present with the people; he has never abandoned them. Now Moses instructs the people that since God has placed his confidence in them, they in turn must give back to God the first fruits of the land. The people are to trust God as God has trusted them.

St. Luke places the famous Gospel story of Jesus' temptation in the desert between the baptism of the Lord and the beginning of his public ministry. Jesus has been commissioned through his baptism, but before he begins his work of building the kingdom on earth, he goes to the desert to have his faith and confidence in the Father tested. Satan tempts Jesus with the three great allurements of our world—power, wealth and prestige. The power of transforming stones to bread, the wealth of the kingdoms of the world, and the prestige of having angels watch over him are all paraded before the Lord. Jesus has complete trust and faith in the Father who sent him to this world to complete an important mission. Jesus has no need for the things of Satan. He already possesses all that he needs. Jesus has the Father's love and guidance and thus is able to withstand the temptations placed before him.

It is sad but unfortunately true that trust is a fleeting virtue in today's world. When present it seems most often to be manifest in the things and people of the world. When evil surrounds us, when the pain, obstacles and difficulties of life weigh us down, where do we turn for help and guidance? Some people seek outlets in alcohol, drugs and other forms of addictive behavior. These only drive us further from the solutions we seek. Others might withdraw from life and give up; still others seek to escape from reality. Some seek answers in the material things of this world alone, with no thought of a higher order.

The story of the botanists and the young lad and our readings today tell us that we who bear the name Christian must place our trust and confidence in God. God is our refuge and strength; he is our helper close at hand. We can have complete confidence in the trustworthiness of God. We know this because of the powerful words of St. Paul in this significant passage from his Letter to the Romans. The Apostle to the Gentiles tells us that if we confess with our lips that Jesus is Lord and believe in our hearts that God raised him from the dead we will be saved. Moreover Paul says, "Everyone who calls on the name of the Lord shall be saved" (Rom 10:13). Thus, we know that God is ever faithful and committed to us. If God is so committed to us that he sent his only-begotten Son to save us, can we not muster the courage to place our hope, trust and confidence in God?

An image might help us to understand our need to trust in God. Picture a small child standing on the edge of a pool. She looks upon the deep water which frightens her because she cannot swim. She begins to cry. Then she raises her eyes, looks out, and sees her mother with arms outstretched. "Jump in," the mother reassures the girl. "There is nothing to fear. I will hold you up." In a similar way Jesus is waiting for us with his arms outstretched. He says, "Have courage; trust in me. Take a chance and jump in; there is nothing to fear. I will keep you from harm." Moreover, he will bring us to eternal life.

Monday Week I

Readings: Leviticus 19:1-2, 11-18;
Matthew 25:31-46

Measuring the Important Things

Each evening, while most people in Washington, D.C. slumber to prepare themselves for another day, a group of workers labor through the night to ready things for tomorrow's business of government. The U.S. government printing office each evening prints the Congressional Record, the complete text of all that was said on the floor of Congress and in the various committees in our complex government structure. Today people complain about gridlock with respect to the legislative branch of government; many people think it accomplishes little. However, careful observers will note that many new laws are passed each legislative session. The mere texts of bills introduced before Congress are daunting in their length and complexity, let alone the debate which accompanies them. While some laws break new ground, others invalidate or repeal existing ordinances; some laws are seldom enforced and serve little function.

Despite the apathy which exists today in regard to the law, our society would suffer chaos without it. At times we view the law as restrictive and concentrate on what it says we cannot do. More thought, however, shows us that law serves to make us free. Without law we would have anarchy which leads to tyranny, the antithesis of freedom.

Yet even with the freedom that law brings, people often ask what is important and necessary when it comes to law. As a people, what do we need to progress and make the world a better place for ourselves now and for future generations?

Today's readings speak about God's law in two different contexts. The Book of Leviticus is filled with laws. The Hebrews regarded the law as the basis of life and of one's relationship with Yahweh. If one obeyed the law then all was right. If one violated it the consequences were clearly spelled out in the Hebrew Scriptures. The laws which God gives to Moses in today's reading all deal with people—how we treat family, friends and members of the community, and what responsibilities we have toward them. Acting honestly and fairly, refusing to bear hatred but rather demonstrating love, summarizes the law.

In the Gospel we hear the familiar story in Matthew of the last judgment. Jesus separates everyone into two categories, the sheep and the goats, and the criterion used to judge people and place them in one group or the other is how they care for one another. Jesus could have emphasized the law to love God above all or stressed the various Hebrew practices of ritual purity and Sabbath observance that made them a people unique to God. But instead the Lord divides people on how they have treated each other. Visiting the sick, feeding the hungry and thirsty, clothing the naked, comforting the sorrowful—only these matter. We will be judged by our adherence to the Golden Rule, love of God and love of neighbor.

Like our nation which makes all kinds of laws, some which are consciously observed and others which are ignored, so the Scriptures are filled with many laws and practices that call for our attention. In the Gospel Jesus says that he has not come to abolish the law but to fulfill it. The Lord came to complete or perfect the law, and he did so by demonstrating the importance of the spirit of the law, lived most powerfully by how we treat one another. As we continue our Lenten trek home may we be mindful of what is truly important. The crown of God's visible creation is the human race, made in the Lord's own image and likeness. Let us show love and respect for all people; let us welcome others as we would welcome God, today and to eternal life.

Tuesday Week I

Readings: Isaiah 55:10-11; Matthew 6:7-15

God's Word Sustains Us

"Sticks and stones may break my bones, but words can never hurt me." We might remember our mothers telling us this when someone said something to hurt us. The expression is correct insofar as words cannot bring physical harm, and for children it has a soothing effect which can often take away the sting and power of insults. When we grow older, however, we realize that the expression simply falls apart, for words possess great power to bring about both good and evil. Words may not land us in a doctor's office or a hospital bed, but they can produce powerful effects which influence decisions and change our world.

Words have been used to inspire others to reach great heights. When Thomas Jefferson wrote the *Declaration of Independence*, including the phrase, "all men are created equal," he set the tone for freedom and democracy which are hallmarks of American society. John F. Kennedy inspired a generation of young Americans to act for others in his inaugural speech: "Ask not what your country can do for you; ask what you can do for your country." In his famous "I Have a Dream" speech in August 1963, Martin Luther King, Jr. inspired African-Americans to work by peaceful means for justice and equality.

The power of words has also been used to generate and promote negative attitudes in our society. Adolph Hitler poisoned the minds of millions of people by his powerful oratory which inflamed latent anti-Semitism. In the everyday world words can boost people and make them feel important or they can rip and tear them to shreds. The power of words must be used prudently.

God's word is the most powerful of all. It challenges, comforts, raises our minds intellectually, and answers many of the questions which life provokes. As Isaiah says in the first reading, God's word is like rain which waters the earth, making it fertile and fruitful. God's word is effective and accomplishes its purpose. As the Letter to the Hebrews says, it is "a two-edged sword," which divides and separates (cf. Heb 4:12); it forces us to make decisions for God or for the world. Jesus knew the power of words and he did not use them idly. Rather, he utilized them to instruct, admonish and praise; he used words to announce the Good News. When the apostles asked him how to pray, Jesus gave them a few powerful words which distill the essence of prayer. Each phrase of the Lord's Prayer is filled with meaning, power and possibility. Most of us recite this prayer many times each day, but do we appreciate and understand what we say? Jesus asks that we praise God's name, build the kingdom of God now, ask for our daily sustenance, and forgive as we are forgiven. That is a full slate, but it comprises the essentials of what being a Christian demands.

Along the road home to God we will meet many situations in which the power of words can make a difference. A thoughtful word at the right moment can make all the difference in the world. Years ago in grade school a teacher once told us, "Engage mind before putting mouth in gear." Those words have carried me through several situations where carelessness in speech could have been fatal. Our words can water and nourish or they can scorch and kill; the choice is ours. Let us use the power of words wisely so as to further God's kingdom on earth this day.

Wednesday Week I

Readings: Jonah 3:1-10; Luke 11:29-32

Accepting God's Messengers

Most people would have to agree that they dislike being told what to do. Each person has a strong streak of independence which rebels when one is told to do things that are disagreeable, difficult or challenging. Sometimes we must refuse to do what others want, especially when we are told to do something that violates our conscience, Christian principles, or who we are as a human person. Often, however, our refusal to do what others want relates to our stubbornness, pride or simple disobedience. Reward greatly motivates us to get things done. If we know that our actions or words will lead where we want to go, whether that be a promotion, pay raise, or first-string position on the basketball team, then we become highly motivated. We produce results regardless of personal pain and sadly, sometimes we even compromise our principles.

Rebelling against what others ask has been with the human race from the dawn of time. Jonah went on a mission which at the outset he did not want. God asked him to go and preach to the people of Nineveh, but Jonah's initial reaction was to run away from the job. God persisted, however, and coerced the reluctant prophet, sending a whale to capture and return him for his mission. I am sure that the Ninevites did not want to hear Jonah's words of doom and destruction, but they heeded the message and changed their ways so quickly that God repented of the evil that was planned for the city and did not carry it out. Jonah's warning motivated the Ninevites to reform.

In the Gospel Jesus is distressed and disappointed at the crowds who demand a sign. They can't see God's presence in him, nor do they recall how the Ninevites repented. They do not want to listen to his message and fail to recognize the power of God present before them. Even Jesus' warning that the present generation would be condemned seems to evoke no reaction from the people; they simply do not want to be told what to do.

Contemporary prophets speak God's word, with its challenges, difficulties and complexities. Are we listening or do we also resist being told what to do? Oscar Romero challenged the rich and powerful, within the Church structure and outside it, with a message that the Gospel requires justice for the poor. Martin Luther King, Jr. and Mahatma Gandhi asked us to see that nonviolence is the way to effect change, within ourselves and in society. Mother Teresa continues to amaze the world and draw men and women to her arduous way of life by telling us that society has the wrong priorities. We need to listen to today's prophets and heed their message. Obedience may not bring us a physical reward, but if this is the only reason that we act then our Christian faith means nothing. We work today to make a better world for all, but our life with God, our road home, must be our chief concern. Let us follow God's prophets today, heed their message, and in the end find eternal life.

Thursday Week I

Readings: Esther C:12, 14-16, 23-25; Matthew 7:7-12

Total Reliance on God

The famous Swedish scientist and inventor of dynamite, Alfred Nobel, lived in luxury with hardly a care in the world. He had grown wealthy from his invention, which was used both to aid society, through its use in construction, and to destroy it, by its application in bombs, projectiles and other weapons of war. His fortune increased when oil was discovered on land he owned in Russia. Nobel cared little for others; he had everything that he needed—or so he thought.

One day he picked up the morning paper and a banner headline shocked him: "Dynamite King Dies." The report was erroneous for Nobel was alive and well, but he was curious to know what others would think of him after his death. The article spoke of Nobel's accomplishments and his place in the higher echelons of society, but when it came to his association with dynamite the article called him "the merchant of death." The comment stung Nobel; he was not sure what to do or how to react. He had always placed his faith in himself and his own ability to get things done, but this new challenge required a different approach. After reflecting for some time Nobel began to realize that he had placed all his hope in his reputation, which he had always believed would be revered after his death. But the article showed him that his idea of himself differed greatly from that of others. He knew at that moment that he needed a new approach to life.

Nobel did not waste time once he realized he had to change. He wanted to contribute to society and leave a positive legacy for posterity. Thus, he changed his will and left his great fortune in a trust to be administered by a board which after his death would award prizes for excellence in scholarship and research. Nobel wanted to recognize people for their contributions to society. So the Nobel Prizes were first awarded in 1901, in five areas: medicine, physics, chemistry, literature and peace.

Alfred Nobel learned the hard way what our readings clearly tell us—we must rely on God. Queen Esther realized that she and her people needed God. In the beautiful prayer which we hear in the first reading she seeks God's assistance in reversing the ill fortunes of her people. She asks God for the strength and courage that she will need in order to carry out her plan, which will bring life to the Hebrews and death to those who seek their extermination.

In the Gospel Jesus asks us to place all our hope in God. In words familiar to us he says, "Ask, and it will be given you; search, and you will find; knock, and the door will be opened for you" (Mt 7:7). God promises that those who turn to him for their needs will receive all that is necessary for life. God, the Creator of all things, will never abandon his greatest creation, the human race. We may tend to go it alone and place our trust in that which is tangible, but we who bear the name Christian must seek a higher order, where we move beyond ourselves and that which we can see to the realm of faith and that which cannot be seen.

Along the road that leads to God we are often tempted to seek the immediate solution which can often translate into self-reliance. We are not content to wait for God to act; we want answers now. But Esther's faith and her knowledge that only God could solve her dilemma prefigured Jesus' words in the Gospel to place our confidence in God. Let us have the courage to rely on God. We couldn't be in better hands.

Friday Week I

Readings: Ezekiel 18:21-28; Matthew 5:20-26

Our Vocation to Holiness

When people today, especially Roman Catholics, hear the word "vocation," their minds turn to priesthood and religious life. It is true that these specific ways of following the Lord are a vocation, but we must expand our horizons to see that vocation more generally applies to all God's people. Each person has a different but equally important role in following the Lord. Most people find their vocation in the working world as educators, engineers, doctors, nurses, service workers, or in a host of other important professions. Many of these people also find their vocation in marriage and family life. Some people simply remain single and still others vow themselves to the celibate life. Despite our differences all Christians have at least two common vocations—to lead lives of service and holiness. These two common denominators of discipleship cannot be avoided; they are integral to who we are as members of God's family.

The readings today describe our common call to holiness and the demands which it places on us. The prophet Ezekiel tells us that God asks us to lead a virtuous life. Some people find virtue while young and others find it later in life. It seems unfair, as the prophet says, for God to punish the one who demonstrates virtue but then falls away, and extol the person who finds conversion. We think it unfair due to our limited way of thinking. We must always remember that our ways are not the ways of God, nor is our timetable the same as the Lord's. The important thing to understand is that God asks us to live the virtuous life. How one comes to this realization, whether it happens from the outset or is found later, seems immaterial to the Lord. What matters is to find virtue and to persevere in living a holy life.

In the Gospel Jesus indicates that our common vocation to holiness will not be easy, but it will require our constant vigilance. The Lord speaks forcefully about our need to be reconciled with our brothers and sisters. He goes beyond the written Mosaic law to say that anger and abusive language toward another violates our call to holiness and must be eliminated from our lives. If anything stands between ourselves and our fellow disciples on the road, we must stop what we are doing and find reconciliation before we may continue. The sense of urgency in this task is clear when Jesus says, "Lose no time."

The demands of everyday life challenge our Christian call to holiness. It is easy to become so embroiled in the day-to-day experiences of our lives, which call for us to perform and produce, that we forget our need to live in the love and light of the Lord. We may do many things, find success, reach great heights, and be feted by the outside world for who we are and what we do. But if this recognition conflicts with our call to holiness and, as Jesus indicates in the Gospel, our need to be reconciled with one another, then we have missed the whole point of our Christian call. What the world considers important may make us wealthy and famous in this life, but if it draws us away from God and our call to holiness then it is truly worthless. Today we are challenged, as we continue our journey home to God, to act virtuously in what we do and say and thereby live our vocation to be holy people. May we live today and each day in the presence of the Lord.

Saturday Week I

Readings: Deuteronomy 26:16-19; Matthew 5:43-48

Our Contract with God

All of us are familiar with contracts of one sort or another. Most of the work that is done these days and many of the things we buy are negotiated through contracts. Sometimes without knowing it, contracts are made in our day-to-day interactions with people. A contract is an agreement between two or more parties whereby each is responsible for certain goods or services that contribute to the benefit of all parties concerned. With rare exceptions today, people are under contract where they live. Whether we own a home or rent our lodging, contracts regulate the agreement to pay a prescribed fee to a bank, lending agency or a landlord. Contracts are made to buy expensive items. Today one is rarely fortunate enough to be able to purchase a car without making extended payments. We agree to pay promptly and regularly while the dealer agrees to provide a good product which is free from defect and performs as advertised. If both parties are faithful to their end of the agreement, then the contract functions well and helps all concerned.

Contracts come in less formal ways; there need be no piece of paper or legal note which says we owe another our money or time. A married couple has an important contract which is written in their hearts. Both parties promise fidelity and love. We make an unwritten contract every time we say that we will help someone, be present at a function or agree to support a project or candidate. Such contracts may be the most difficult in that there is little at risk if we fail in our obligations. If we don't make the house or car payment we run the risk of repossession. Written contracts are legal documents and, therefore, command our attention because of our system of laws. But if we fail another human being, if we forget our agreement to love or to be present, the consequences somehow don't seem to be as acute, until our lack of faithfulness ruptures relationships.

Our readings speak to us of the great contract between God and his people and the goal we must seek in this agreement. God made the first contract with the human race through the Hebrew people. Our ancestors in faith were given a special opportunity to be a people uniquely God's own. The contract was both written and unwritten. The written law, the Decalogue or Ten Commandments, was a pattern of life which God asked the people to follow. God first promised fealty and love to all the people, pledging to be present and aid them at all times. God would raise the Hebrew nation above all others. In response the Hebrews were to be loyal to God and to observe the statutes and decrees of the Decalogue. God's contract with the Hebrews was written on their hearts as well, for their relationship with God was unique among all people.

In the Gospel Jesus speaks of the goal of the contract, "Be perfect, therefore, as your heavenly Father is perfect" (Mt 5:48). That is quite a demanding standard. But God does not ask this without giving us the tools to make it happen. Jesus realizes our weaknesses for he experienced temptation and every human emotion, but he also knows that we can rise above temptation if we make the effort. Jesus showed us how to live, giving us the example to follow in our contract with God.

Our contract with God was first made at our baptism, but it is renewed on a regular basis. God agreed to be present and to never abandon us. As members of the Church we also gained special status and privilege through the power of the sacraments and the opportunities afforded by the Christian community. On our part, whether we knew it or not, baptism required us to return our time, expertise and resources to God. Our contract with the Lord is not written on paper but is written on our hearts. Its legality in the world is not obvious and thus we often are unfaithful to it. We say that we'll get back to it; we'll take time for God someday.

God is ever faithful; we must respond in turn to the love first shown us. Our contract with God, if lived well, brings dividends now and later. Living in the presence of the Lord raises our minds and hearts to new heights; we feel good about who we are and what we can accomplish. We begin to truly believe that with God all things are possible. The final episode of our contract with God is still to be experienced, but we have God's promise that it will be spectacular. St. Paul writes, "No eye has seen, nor ear heard, nor the human heart conceived, what God has prepared for those who love him" (1 Cor 2:9). Let us always remember our contract with God, which aids us today and tomorrow brings us to eternal life.

Meditations for the Second Week of Lent

Sunday Week II (A)

Readings: Genesis 12:1-4;
2 Timothy 1:8-10; Matthew 17:1-9

Allowing God to Change Us

"Hoke, you are my best friend." It took Daisy Werthan almost twenty years to make that statement. The relationship between Daisy and Hoke was rocky at the outset. Daisy had driven her beautiful 1948 Packard into her neighbor's backyard. Boolie Werthan, Daisy's son, thought that such an incident indicated that his mother should stop driving and get a chauffeur. Boolie hired Hoke Coleburn, a middle aged African-American, for the job. Daisy, however, would not accept this change in her life; she was not open to being transformed.

Boolie may have hired Hoke but that did not mean that Miss Daisy had to use him. As Hoke stood idly by, Miss Daisy took the streetcar wherever she went, whether to the hair dresser or the grocery store. Hoke Coleburn was being paid for doing nothing, which was exactly how Miss Daisy wanted things.

As stubborn as she could be, Miss Daisy ultimately did change her attitude. One day she needed a few things from the store. She left the house and began to walk toward the streetcar. Hoke decided that Miss Daisy's refusal to use his services needed to end. As she walked down the sidewalk Hoke slowly drove alongside in the new 1948 Hudson that Boolie had purchased for his mother. "Where are you going?" scowled Daisy. Hoke replied, "I'm fixin' to take you to the store!" Although still unhappy with the arrangement, Daisy agreed to get into the car. Her conversion had begun.

Despite Daisy's resistance, Hoke had become her chauffeur. Whether it was to the synagogue, the store, or a trip to Mobile to visit relatives, Daisy and Hoke went together. As the years passed their relationship as driver and passenger grew into a close bond. Then one day Miss Daisy's conversion was complete. The process had been long and difficult, but now it was finished. Her conversion was her statement of faith, "Hoke, you are my best friend."

Alfred Uhry's 1988 Pulitzer Prize winning play and popular movie, *Driving Miss Daisy*, is more than a story of a chauffeur and an elderly rich widow. It is a story of the process of transformation and acceptance in one's life. During the season of Lent our readings challenge us with this same message of renewal.

In our first reading from Genesis we hear how God asked Abram to go forth, to venture out, to change and be converted. What God asked of Abram could not have been easy. He was an old man, yet he was asked to leave his home, his livelihood, everything that he knew. God had given him a promise, a special blessing, that one day he would be the father of a great nation. Even with such a promise, however, Abram would not have been able to act if he had not been a man of faith. Abram believed that God was calling him to change for some good reason.

The Gospel story of Jesus' transfiguration is another example of transformation. Theologians debate about this passage in Scripture. Some say it was an actual event;

some think it was a special spiritual experience of the apostles. Some theologians think the story is a misplaced post-resurrection account of how the apostles experienced Jesus. All three synoptic Gospels tell us about this event in Jesus' life. This fact alone makes this passage highly significant. What is its importance? When Jesus was transfigured, his clothes became a dazzling white, and his physical appearance radiated glory. The transformation which occurred with the three favored apostles, Peter, James and John, was most significant. Their experience of seeing Jesus transfigured changed their lives forever.

Lent is a time to allow change, to welcome the opportunity to be transformed. We can look at the three traditional disciplines of Lent and see how they can help us along the path which leads to renewal in our lives. Almsgiving is the first discipline. We need to believe that works of mercy are necessary. How can we change our schedules or daily lives so as to make almsgiving something that is possible in what we do? Do we need to change any attitudes about almsgiving which may deter us from it?

Fasting is the second discipline. Do we need to change our eating habits—permanently? Do we need to eliminate certain items from our life, things which ultimately cause us harm—drugs, drink, tobacco? Can we transform our lives to be in solidarity with those who lack the material possessions we enjoy?

Prayer is the third traditional discipline of Lent. Can we change our priorities if needed so as to assure we make time for conversation with God today and every day? Are we willing to try new methods of prayer in order to make our prayer more fruitful and fulfilling? Can we let the word of God become part of us, to enter deep down so as to later blossom forth as God's love directed toward others?

Each day we have the opportunity to meet the Lord. During our Lenten journey may the encounters we have with God change our hearts. Let us accept the change that God asks of us, as Abram did, as Miss Daisy did in Alfred Uhry's play. May our encounter with God change us forever!

Sunday Week II (B)

Readings: Genesis 22:1-2, 9-13, 15-18; Romans 8:31-34; Mark 9:2-10

Reliance on God

The famous Greek dramatist Sophocles graced the world with his many plays. His famous trilogy of *Oedipus Rex, Oedipus at Colonnus* and *Antigone* is his greatest legacy. This trilogy has a famous section known as the riddle of the Sphinx. To gain entry to his desired destination, Oedipus must solve this famous riddle. The passage is as follows: what has four legs in the morning, two legs in the afternoon and three legs in the evening? The answer is a human being. In the morning, the first period of our life, we crawl; we need four legs to move and get around. In the great middle or afternoon of our life we walk upright on two legs. In the twilight of our life we again need some assistance, such as a cane or a helping hand; we use three legs then.

The riddle of the sphinx tells us something powerful about our reliance on others. As infants we need the support of others. As young children we are totally dependent on others for food, clothing, shelter, love—all our needs. As children we trust that all will be provided. We don't worry; our trust is absolute in those who care for us. When we are old enough to walk, we then begin to rely on ourselves. We venture out, just a little at first, but later with ever bolder steps. We try things for ourselves. As time goes on our ability to trust in others begins to wane. Life throws us curves; we get knocked down and kicked around. Our trust shifts to a more exclusive reliance on the tangible and visible things of our world. We begin to say that we need to do it ourselves since we cannot rely on others any longer. They just might not come through for us! When we get older, when we need that third leg, we again begin to trust in others. We can no longer do everything that we once could do. We need the aid of other people, for the complex and sometimes even the simple everyday tasks of life.

Today's readings, like the riddle of the Sphinx, tell us something about relying on others, especially on God. In the first reading we hear about Abraham and Isaac. Abraham was an adult; he could walk properly and speak for himself. Yet with complete reliance Abraham placed his whole life in God's hands; he had total faith. Our reading today gives us only a summary of a longer story—there is more to know. God told Abraham that he would be the father of a great nation. Isaac was Abraham and Sarah's only child, the fruit of their old age. God is asking Abraham to sacrifice his one chance for an heir. For three days Abraham and his son Isaac journeyed, yet Abraham's faith never wavered. In the end he received his reward as the father of a great nation. Today the Jewish people still see Abraham as their father in faith.

In the second reading we hear about the obedience of Jesus to God the Father. Jesus was human, like you and me, yet his trust in the Father, unlike ours, never vacillated. Jesus was obedient to God to the point of death on the cross. Because of his obedience Jesus was exalted and has become for us, as Paul says, the great intercessor with God. This is why all the prayers of the Mass end with, "we ask this" or "we pray this through Christ our Lord." Jesus' reliance on God was complete and total.

Conversion is necessary if we are to rely totally on the Lord. Jesus is transfigured before the apostles. He is changed in appearance but this transformation is only temporary. The more important conversion is found with the apostles. Peter, James and John were always there, it seems, when important events happened in the life of the early Church. These men were converted on the inside, where it counts, to a life of total reliance on God. Certainly the apostles failed; they had their problems. But their faith in and obedience to Jesus became a part of their being. They were changed forever.

If we were asked upon whom or what do we rely, what would be our honest answer? Some would answer that they rely on the material things of this life. Being tangible, we know for certain they exist, and that we can rely on them—at least so it seems. Some people rely on others in their life, whether family, friends or associates. Some rely totally on themselves.

All of us to a lesser or greater extent need to be converted to a complete and unqualified trust in God. Abraham relied on God and became the father of a great nation. Jesus relied on the Father and was exalted to glory. If we rely on God and have complete faith, then we too will find the rewards of God.

Let us follow the example of Abraham and Jesus. Let us not be dominated by the world, as the riddle of the Sphinx suggests. Let us hope and pray that if the world placed us on trial for our faith and reliance on God there would be sufficient evidence to convict us!

Sunday Week II (C)

Readings: Genesis 15:5-12, 17-18; Philippians 3:17–4:1; Luke 9:28-36

Transformed in the Lord

"I'd sell my soul to play for the Washington Senators!" shouts Joe Hardy, the protagonist in the popular Broadway musical *Damn Yankees.* Joe is what we call today your average middle-age "couch potato." He sits in front of his television and watches baseball. Most of the time his beloved team the Senators are defeated by "those damn New York Yankees." Joe had always wanted to play ball but things just did not work out that way. Marriage, children and work comprised his life. Thus, one day in frustration he declares he would sell his soul to play for the Senators. It just so happens that the devil is listening to Joe and appears quite suddenly in his living room. Satan makes a deal with the middle-aged man. The devil will transform him into the young strapping athlete he once was, so that he can play for the Senators, but when the season is over Joe's soul will belong to the devil. After a moment of thought Joe agrees and he is instantly transformed into a young man.

Joe manages to get a try-out with the Senators and the manager is quite impressed. Soon Joe is making newspaper headlines as a star and the Senators begin to move up in the standings. As the season nears its close the Yankees and Senators are neck and neck for the pennant and a chance to go to the World Series. Joe has made a great contribution, but his heart misses his old existence, his family and friends at work. He begins to think about how he might get out of his pact with the devil.

The whole season comes down to one final game; whoever wins goes to the Series. The last game between the Senators and Yankees comes down to the last inning and ultimately the last out. Joe is playing center field for the home team Senators who are ahead by one run. A crack of the bat sends Joe racing toward the fence. As he runs back he begins to revert to the middle-aged couch potato that he really is. The devil is upset that Joe has broken his pact and wants to return to his old existence. A middle-aged man again, Joe still manages to lumber back and make the catch, crashing through the centerfield fence in the process. He runs for fear that others will discover who he truly is; he was changed in body but not in heart.

Joe Hardy's transformation in *Damn Yankees* was external. On the inside, however, he never changed and thus he returned to his old way of life. Our readings today speak of our need to be transformed on the inside where we can experience a permanent conversion to the Lord.

In the Gospel we hear how Peter, James and John, the three apostles who always seem to be present at the most important times, go up the mountain with Jesus. They witness the Lord's physical transformation, his transfiguration. His clothes became a dazzling white; the whole scene is beyond human description. Jesus' new appearance mesmerizes the apostles. According to Luke, Peter is so powerfully struck by the experience that he does not know what he is saying. The story of the transfiguration tells us what happened to Jesus. But a more important question for us is: what happened to those three apostles? We know they were amazed, but did the vision change them on the inside in some permanent way? Certainly the experience changed their view of Jesus forever; they would always see him in another light. Not only did they see the Lord's transfigured body, but they heard a voice from heaven say, "This is my Son, my Chosen; listen to him" (Lk 9:35). Jesus was transfigured, but his temporary physical transformation produced a permanent change of heart for the apostles.

Lent is our time to be renewed. We can change everything about our physical appearance, but this does not truly transform us. Our clothes, hairstyle and weight may change, but this is transitory, not lasting. What we must seek is a permanent conversion on the inside, one which changes us forever.

Our encounters with God must renew our lives. By keeping our perspective of who we are and where we want to go, our experience of God can change us. Paul says to the Philippians in today's second reading that Christ will transform us if we will stand firm in the Lord. In our busy world, which daily seems to demand more of our time and energy, we are tempted to cast aside our faith and to place God somewhere down the priority list. This, however, cannot be an option for those who bear the name Christian. If God is not our first priority at all times, then we have missed our call and the opportunities that it brings.

Joe Hardy wanted to be transformed, but he could achieve this only externally; his heart was not changed.

He never sought a conversion of the heart, which for Joe was providential; the devil never had a chance with him. We may not be so lucky. We must be transformed on the inside to a new and deeper understanding of our role in God's loving plan of salvation. May all the opportunities we have to encounter God, people and events in the highs and the lows of life, transform us so that we may live more fully in the presence of the Lord.

Monday Week II

Readings: Daniel 9:4-10; Luke 6:36-38

Handing on the Compassion of God

In the first years of the 16th century Spain was at war with France. Ignatius, a brave and loyal Spanish soldier, was on his way to fame and fortune in the military. Nominally a Christian by baptism, he rarely took time for God but focused his attention on other things. This all changed during the siege of Pamploma on May 20, 1520 when shrapnel from a cannon ball almost tore off his right leg. Confined to a hospital bed for a long period of recuperation, he was forced to think about his life. Few books were available in those days so Ignatius read what was provided—a life of Christ and a book on the lives of the saints. Ignatius began to realize that there was much more to life than his narrow personal needs and desires, that God had bigger and better plans for the world and for him. His reading changed his whole perspective and he decided to move his life in another direction.

After he left the hospital Ignatius began the long road back to God. He first had to believe that God could and would forgive him, a feat which he accomplished through prayer and reflection at Manresa. His peace of mind was restored and he began to write the ideas which would later be the foundation of the *Spiritual Exercises.* Once Ignatius believed himself to be reconciled he knew that the next step was to share his fortune with others. In 1534, at the age of 33, he gathered together six others who vowed to live in chastity and poverty and, if possible, to go to the Holy Land. If such a pilgrimage could not be conducted the men would place themselves at the service of the Pope. Since circumstances made the pilgrimage impossible, they decided to go to Rome. Eventually Pope Paul III gave canonical approval to this fledgling band of religious who called themselves the Society of Jesus, commonly known as the Jesuits. Their task was to pass on the compassion and love of God to all they encountered.

I am sure that St. Ignatius of Loyola read more than once the beautiful prayer from the Book of Daniel presented in our reading. The Hebrews had sinned against God, and the punishment for their many failures was exile to Babylon. In anguish the people raise this special prayer to seek God's mercy, compassion and forgiveness. They realize that they have failed to heed the warnings of the prophets who spoke God's word. Yet the people believe in God's mercy and call out for it.

In the Gospel Jesus tells us that the compassion we receive must be shared with others. Only by passing on the love and mercy of God can we fully experience its power in our own lives. God's love and forgiveness are too great for any of us to accept alone. Moreover, God does not give us gifts to be hoarded but rather to be shared with all we meet. We must respond to the God who first loved us by aiding, sharing with, and loving God's people. As Jesus says in the Gospel, "Give, and it will be given to you. A good measure, pressed down, shaken together, running over, will be put into your lap; for the measure you give will be the measure you get back" (Lk 6:38).

Lent gives us a great opportunity to move from being lukewarm in our faith to catching a fire that can inflame others. Experiencing the magnanimous power of God's love and forgiveness will inflame us to share our knowledge and belief in Christ with others. The lives of saints such as Ignatius of Loyola show us how to pass on the goodness given us by God. Today share a smile, a kind word, an ear of compassion with another. Let us pass on God's love!

Tuesday Week II

Readings: Isaiah 1:10, 16-20; Matthew 23:1-12

Working Behind the Scenes for God

During the first half of the 19th century in the United States the scourge of slavery created wounds in American society that still fester today. The buying and selling of human beings and their forced work as chattel was an atrocity almost beyond human understanding. Yet we know from our reading of history that slavery was an accepted practice, not only in the United States, but in other places and at different times throughout history. Some people and groups worked on the frontlines to banish this practice from our shores. William Lloyd Garrison led an abolitionist movement which was highly visible, demanded action, and stirred the hearts of many to conversion.

Harriet Tubman was little known in her day except to those she saved and those who pursued her. She was one of the principal "conductors" on the American underground railroad system, the secret organization which aided Southern slaves in their flight to freedom. In the ten years prior to the Civil War Harriet Tubman made at least fifteen forays into the slave territory of Southern Maryland, her birthplace. She rescued her brothers and sisters who suffered, as she had, from the lash of the slave master. Nothing could deter her, even when a large bounty was offered for her capture. She did not make headlines, but effectively worked behind the scenes to rescue God's people.

In the Gospel Jesus speaks of the contrast between people who do things to gain marks of respect in public and those who act simply to serve others. Jesus urges us to walk the path of humility, not seeking praise, but being content with leading lives of service. Moreover, Jesus says that the greatest person will be the one who serves the rest.

The road that leads home to God holds many lessons for us. We know, as Isaiah suggests, that it is necessary to wash ourselves clean, to set things right. God will be with us; if we follow and obey we shall eat the good things of the land. But our need for reconciliation, like that of service, doesn't have to be a public affair. We can be just as effective by working behind the scenes. Recognition is an important element of human self-worth; we need to know that we are important and useful. But the ultimate recognition we should strive for is to be singled out by God for how we have done his work and built his kingdom. When compared with inheriting eternal life, all other forms of recognition fade into insignificance.

We may not have a role as hidden as that of Harriet Tubman, but working behind the scenes with little recognition will be the normal course for most. Let us rejoice that God has chosen us to carry on Jesus' message of love and peace to a world which so desperately needs his presence. As Jesus says, "Rejoice and be glad, for your reward is great in heaven" (Mt 5:12).

Wednesday Week II

Readings: Jeremiah 18:18-20; Matthew 20:17-28

Serving God by Serving One Another

Pierre Toussaint is not well known in Catholic circles today. This is our loss, for in 19th century New York he was outstanding for serving God by serving those most in need. Toussaint was born in Santo Domingo in 1766. As an indentured servant, he emigrated to New York City in 1787, when the new United States of America declared victory in the Revolutionary War. He became a hairdresser, which earned him a handsome salary and access to the rich and powerful people in the city. In 1807 Toussaint was made a free man. With the money he had made, he purchased the freedom of his sister and the woman whom he would later marry. At this time he began his ministry of charitable activity, becoming a great benefactor of orphanages, Catholic schools and other institutions. He also assisted individuals, including many priests who seemed on the verge of pauperism. Toussaint nursed the victims of the frequent epidemics which swept through the city due to unsanitary and crowded living conditions. He began each day with Mass at 6 AM and then, renewed in spirit, assisted others through his many charitable works. Pierre Toussaint was a servant who found joy in doing God's work.

Service is an integral part of the common Christian vocation to holiness and discipleship. Long before Jesus, the great prophets like Jeremiah, from whom we hear today, understood their challenge in bringing God's word to all people. To be a prophet in Israel was a difficult task, requiring not only special gifts of speech but almost heroic courage. Jeremiah realizes that the citizens of Jerusalem have contrived a plot to bring about his downfall and death. He cries out to God, asking to be remembered for the service that he gave in speaking God's word and helping people to turn from evil in their lives. Jeremiah was a public servant of God and through this life found the path that would lead him home.

In today's Gospel, the mother of Zebedee's sons asks for a favor that is much more than assistance or even a promise for the future; she asks for an eternal promise for her sons. Probably most of us, knowing Jesus to be God's Son, would have been mortified or at least shocked at her boldness. Jesus takes it all in stride and uses the opportunity, as he always does, to teach the people a valuable lesson: "Whoever wishes to be great among you must be your servant" (Mt 20:26). As Jesus came to serve, so must we serve God and one another.

Most Christians contribute to society in many ways, from business and professional work to politics, athletics and religion. The attitude we take in our tasks raises our actions from being simply work to that of ministry. When we use our expertise, time and resources for the service of God's people, then we participate in the process which builds the kingdom of God in our world. If done well, service and ministry make our daily tasks a bit simpler because we have a greater motivation for what we do. If our attitude is that of a servant, then we know that in little and greater ways we contribute to the needs of others and thereby bring the presence of God to the person, situation or event. Let us rejoice that we have been called to serve and believe that it is in service that we find the path which leads us home to God.

Thursday Week II

Readings: Jeremiah 17:5-10; Luke 16:19-31

Place Your Trust in God

During my novitiate year in Cascade, Colorado, eight miles west of Colorado Springs, I had the opportunity to minister in a Catholic hospital as a member of the pastoral care team. Each Tuesday I spent the day visiting patients, glad to be away from the confinement and isolation which the novitiate experience requires. My mentor at the hospital was an older nun, Sister Melithon. After a long career in education, she was now ministering in the hospital. She took me under her wing and gave me much direction and encouragement. One day when I arrived she took me aside, as was her custom, to brief me on those patients she wanted me to visit. The previous afternoon a young man had been brought to the hospital as a result of a motorcycle accident. Before the incident he was a healthy and energetic man of twenty-one years who had many friends, a good job and future plans; he was even engaged to be married. Now he lay in a hospital bed paralyzed from the neck down. The doctor's preliminary examination was inconclusive, but if recovery was possible it would be a long and tedious process.

Sister Melithon asked me to visit the young man and his family who were gathered, still in shock at the events of the previous day. I agreed to the assignment, but with no sense of what I should do or what would happen. As I entered the room stillness and tension hung heavily on it;

a certain sense of gloom pervaded it despite the bright sun that shone through the window. Only after a minute or so did the family in any way acknowledge my presence. The silence continued as I stood with the family around their loved one who lay immobile, his head and neck in traction. Many ideas ran through my mind of what to say or how to act, but none seemed appropriate at the time. It was a time in my life when I was totally powerless. Words were inadequate; the only solution was to be present, say nothing, and allow the power of God to take over. It was a time when I and all present needed to place their trust totally in God.

Each of us has a similar story of situations in life when it seems that anything we do is either inappropriate or empty. We want to do something, but our words and actions cannot convey our heart's desire to help. At these times the power in today's readings becomes clear. Jeremiah says that whoever places trust in human beings is like a barren bush in the desert that enjoys no change of season, but rather stands in a lava waste of salt and empty earth. In a similar way the rich man in today's Gospel story, known traditionally as Dives, who has placed his whole trust in riches, now realizes the error of his way. It is too late for him but there is hope for his brothers—if they will heed the dictates of the Lord. Abraham tells him that they already have what they need to place their confidence in God; Dives has no recourse but to hope that his relatives will perceive it.

Trust in God is essential. If we can place our hope and confidence in the Lord then we, as the prophet says, will be like a tree planted beside the waters which stretches out its roots in all directions. It fears no drought for it can always reach water. Its leaves stay green and it bears fruit at all times because it is firmly planted near the stream.

We must be like the tree planted near the water. God is certainly our lifeline, the one who has given us all things and continues to sustain us each day. Humans want to take control; we think in our modern age that we have solutions for everything. Sometimes the reality hits us when we least expect it and then we feel powerless to act. When nothing human seems to work then we realize our need for God. Let us not wait for this eventuality. Rather, let us turn over our lives to the Lord as we continue along the road which leads us home.

Friday Week II

Readings: Genesis 37:3-4, 12-13, 17-28; Matthew 21:33-43, 45-46

Rejection Leads to Loss

The ideas of Christopher Columbus revolutionized the world, but they were not easily accepted. Growing up in Genoa, Italy, Columbus studied science in a rapidly expanding intellectual environment. Once he came to believe that the earth was a sphere it was a logical conclusion that one could reach the East Indies, with its wealth of spices and other products which Europeans desired, by sailing west. Thus the long and dangerous voyage around Africa and then north to the Indian ports could be avoided. As simple as it appeared we know that Columbus had a difficult time selling his idea to the crown heads of state in Europe. He could not convince his fellow Italians nor did he make a favorable impression on John, the king of Portugal, who had sponsored many of the early voyages of expedition. Ferdinand and Isabella in Spain were Columbus' last resort. They took a chance in accepting his ideas, an opportunity which was rewarded with vast discoveries of land, wealth and peoples. The history of the world would be much different if Columbus' ideas had been accepted by others. Rejecting the possibility resulted in a lost opportunity.

In thinking of rejection, our minds usually turn to the person, group or idea that is not accepted. However, in many cases the true loser in such a case is the person who had the opportunity to say yes, but found the idea unacceptable. Joseph was rejected by his brothers. They envied him because their father, Jacob, favored Joseph as the child of his old age. The colorful coat which Joseph wore was a sign of his favor and it irked his brothers. Their jealousy led them to sell Joseph into slavery. However, as we all know from reading Genesis, he turned the tables, became a ruler in Egypt, and saved his family. By rejecting Joseph his brothers became the great losers.

The Gospel parable speaks of the rejection of God's servants by the Hebrews, especially the priests and elders of the people. Like the sons of Jacob, they are jealous of the son of the vineyard owner, for he will inherit everything. Their plan of murder, which they think will bring them the property they seek, only leads to problems and pain. As Jesus says, "The stone that the builders rejected has become the cornerstone" (Mt 21:42). Because the religious leaders of Israel rejected Jesus and his message they lost out when the kingdom of God was taken from them and given to the Gentiles.

In our daily lives many opportunities arise which provide the possibility to grow, experience new things and stretch our horizons. Unfortunately we often close ourselves off to these possibilities, thus losing out. We reject many people because they are not of the same class, color, religion or ethnic origin. We reject ideas and attitudes because they are new, challenging or different than our own. We reject opportunities because they ask something of us and require us to go beyond ourselves. One cannot accept all opportunities; we must make decisions and choices in our lives. Often, however, we reject things and people out of hand and in the process miss the chance to grow, especially in our spiritual lives. The things we reject may not change history, like the rejection of Columbus, but the opportunity missed will be lost forever. Let us make greater efforts to be accepting, to discover new things, and thus clear a straighter path home to God.

Saturday Week II

Readings: Micah 7:14-15, 18-20;
Luke 15:1-3, 11-32

God's Forgiveness Overflows

A saintly old woman went out one night for a short walk before going to bed. The sky was clear; the stars shown brightly, and a full moon shed its light. The woman was deeply touched as she observed the sky with all its beauty. With a deep sense of the grandeur of God, wonder at God's creative hand, and the realization of her own limited humanity, she fell on her knees and cried out, "O God of infinite goodness, patience and beauty, please don't ever let me offend you in the slightest way again. To know you, love you, and serve you is all that I desire." Then she heard a voice from the heavens say, "My daughter, if I granted this request to everyone, how could I show my infinite mercy, love and forgiveness, which is the clearest way I have to let people know and experience my presence in their lives?"

This story tells us how much God wants to demonstrate love and forgiveness. Like the pious woman, none of us want to offend God; we wish to find holiness in our lives. However, as imperfect human beings it is impossible to maintain a flawless record. At times in our journey to God we will intentionally or accidentally take a detour which may threaten our relationship with the Creator. Despite our imperfections God wants us back; he wants to show mercy and grant forgiveness.

The familiar Gospel passage today, the parable of the prodigal son, could also be called the parable of the forgiving father. It speaks of God's desire to bring us home, for in God's plan no one is intentionally left out. All people are welcome; we must only make the initial effort to turn our minds to God and allow the richness of God's mercy to flow over us like the waters of a stream which continually renew life. The father in the parable, like God, allowed his son to wander off without trying to control the son's actions, errant as they would become. In his wisdom the father realizes that his young son must discover for himself the error of his ways, come to realize his need for others, and then make the conscious decision to return. The father, like God, stands ready with open arms to welcome back his son. Not one word is exchanged between father and son, yet reconciliation has occurred; the father magnanimously forgives his son.

The forgiving father's relationship with his older son also demonstrates God's abiding presence and desire to show love. The elder son storms off and wants nothing to do with his family, but the father says that he has always been with him. It is clear that the father wants to teach his older son that forgiveness is infinitely important, for it allows one to again enjoy the presence of the father which the elder son, without knowing it, has possessed all along.

In writing to the rebellious northern tribes of Israel, the prophet Micah told the people that God was ready to show them mercy. He writes that God "does not retain his anger forever, because he delights in showing clemency. He will again have compassion upon us; he will tread our iniquities under foot" (Mic 7:18-19). God will remain faithful to the covenant as he swore to Abraham.

Reconciliation and a return to the Lord are the people's choice; God always extends the invitation.

With the multiple problems which besiege us, the hustle and bustle of life, and the never-ending demands on our time and person, it is truly consoling to know that God's mercy and forgiveness always surround us. God is always at work to find us and return us to the fold. In his classic poem, *The Hound of Heaven,* Francis Thompson metaphorically describes how God relentlessly pursues those who flee him. Only one thing is required to experience the Lord's mercy and forgiveness—we must express the desire to find it. God asks very little of us. He will do all the work; we merely need to say, "Yes, Lord, I want to return. I do love you."

Reconciliation is an important concept for all who bear the name Christian. The Lenten journey provides an excellent opportunity to discover our need for it and to experience its transforming and healing power. Let us reflect on our need to return to God, in the little ways and possibly the greater. Let us be open to God whose overflowing mercy and forgiveness only ask for our assent.

Meditations for the Third Week of Lent

Sunday Week III (A)

Readings: Exodus 17:3-7; Romans 5:1-2, 5-8; John 4:5-42

The Water of Life

Water is a necessity of life; we cannot live without it. Ancient peoples certainly knew this was true. The Egyptian civilization sprang up along the Nile River, which became the source of life for the people. The river made the desert land fertile and it provided water for food and drink. The Nile was the primary source of transportation as well. The people lived close to the river and they didn't stray far from it. The Mesopotamians built their civilization between two mighty rivers, the Tigris and the Euphrates. The land today is known as the fertile crescent. The water from the rivers provided for these people as the Nile did for the Egyptians. In many ways the river, as a source of water, dictated how these ancient peoples lived their lives.

Water is just as important today as it was in ancient times. Growing up in Southern California, water entered into my daily life. I lived only twenty miles from the ocean, so the beach was a favorite get-away place. When rainfall was sparse water restrictions were enacted due to the large population in the Los Angeles area. During my time in the Navy I was introduced to water in different ways. I experienced the power and danger of the ocean while aboard ships at sea. Mighty storms sometimes arose, including one which almost sank our ship in

December 1979. I've experienced the darkness of the ocean when submerged on a submarine for three or more months at a time.

Our readings today tell us about the necessity of water in our life—not only the water of nature, but the supernatural water of God. The first reading from Exodus paints a picture which we need to visualize. Imagine 600,000 people in a desert without water. We can understand why they were complaining to Moses. The Israelites needed the water of nature to satisfy their bodily needs. God provided for them by giving them the water which sustains life.

In the Gospel Jesus expands the notion of water. The water needed to sustain us comes from the rivers, seas and rains. But Jesus says that we need more. We need a new "living water" which will quench our thirst forever. Jesus asks the Samaritan woman for water in order to enter a dialogue with her. He is not interested in the water that sustains bodily life; he wants to teach the woman, the Samaritans and us about the water that brings spiritual life. Jesus wants the woman to respond to his questions; he wants her to ask for this special water. Jesus tells us that the water he can provide shall become a fountain within each and every person who seeks it.

What is this living water? Some might suggest that the water is wisdom. Some might say the water is grace, faith or even divine life. I think the water of which Jesus speaks is God's love. No doubt God's love can be a fountain which springs forth. We can see the effects of God's love in people each day. This love which is a wellspring, is the same love which allowed Jesus to die for us, as Paul says today, for the sinful of our world, for you and me!

The living water of God's love begins for Christians in the sacrament of Baptism. Through this action we become children of God, children of the light. The living water of God's love becomes a part of us for the first time in a very real and special way. The waters of nature, so needed to sustain life, are replaced by the fountain of living water which is God's love, given to us through the action of Christ in our lives.

During our Lenten journey we especially welcome the catechumens, those who are on a journey toward Baptism. At the same time, however, we are challenged to fulfill our own baptismal commitment. Yes, the Lenten journey culminates in the reception of Christ's living water of Baptism for some. But most of us are challenged to ask: "How does the living water of God's love come forth from us?" Do we believe in the priesthood of the baptized? This is the idea that all are called to service, traditionally the role of the deacon. It means that we are all called to preach and proclaim God's word, normally the role of the priest. The priesthood of the baptized means that we are all called to administer, the traditional role of the bishop. Do we believe that the living water which God gives in Baptism requires something of us? Do we believe that through Baptism we make a commitment, a commitment to God, a commitment to God's people, a commitment to pour forth the fountain of eternal life given to us, to share God's love with others?

Our readings today tell us of two types of water. We hear of the water which sustains and nurtures, the water which we drink and which feeds the land. This is the water from nature. But Jesus today tells us about another water, one which gives life, one which in its supernatural origins blooms forth in God's love for all people. Let us today realize its necessity and see the power of water as experienced in the love of our God for all people.

Sunday Week III (B)

Readings: Exodus 20:1-17;
1 Corinthians 1:22-25; John 2:13-25

The Sign of Faith

Signs govern many aspects of our world. It is impossible to go far on the highway without finding several signs. Some of these signs give direction and distance to destinations we seek; some are cautionary and alert us to dangers; still others give us information about local laws, points of interest along the way, and details such as where we might stay, get a good meal or fill our gas tank. As we drive we generally encounter many billboards which are a different kind of sign. These signs tell us all sorts of information, advertise for many assorted products, and give us all the facts on the latest sales, fads and happenings in the local area.

Although not as visible or readily apparent, another type of sign can be equally informative and even more important for our lives. We often can see, feel or interpret the signs of weather. A sudden chill, a breeze that blows from a specific direction or ominous clouds on the horizon speak to us from our experience and indicate what the day will bring. Some weather signs have even been "immortalized" by Scripture. People at sea know well the adage based on the Gospel, "Red sky in the morning, sailor take warning. Red sky at night, sailor's delight" (cf. Mt 16:2-3). Non-tangible signs are experienced through the events of the day. We hear people speak of "the signs of the times." The rising crime rate, different views of life held by youth and adults, and a higher cost of living are only three examples that speak of the times in which we live. There is also the providential sign. When things happen one way, usually different from what we had anticipated, we say, "It is a sign from God."

Signs, both physical and experiential, are best understood as occurrences of faith. Our readings today speak of how the signs of faith have changed over time, but each one demonstrates the presence of God in our lives. The Hebrews in the desert needed a sign that God was with them on their trek to the Promised Land. The great plagues of Egypt were behind them; they needed something new. Thus, God provided them with a sign of his covenant with the people, the Decalogue or Ten Commandments. The law became a great sign, something which the people could grasp. It enabled them to say that they belonged, that they had a unique and special relationship with God.

When God became incarnate in the person of Jesus, the sign of faith became the Lord himself. As we hear in the Gospel the people demand a sign to show them that Jesus has the authority to do what he does, but the Lord simply replies that he is the sign. Unfortunately the people do not recognize who Christ is and thus miss the sign of the presence of God in their midst.

Writing after Jesus' death and resurrection, St. Paul asks the people to find a new source of the sign of faith. With the Lord no longer physically present in the world, the sign of faith must be in our memory of and belief in Jesus, who he was and what he taught. To some, such as the Jews and Gentiles, the sign of Jesus' salvific death is an absurdity, but to those who believe, it is the power and wisdom of God (cf. 1 Cor 1:23-24).

Signs of God's presence which nurture our faith surround us. There is the beauty of nature which at times overpowers our senses with color, fragrance, power and majesty. We have the sign of one another. We are, as Genesis says, made in the image and likeness of God and thus we are the presence or sign of God to one another. We also have the grace of this season of Lent as a special sign of our need to prepare as we travel the road home to God. All of the signs we encounter and utilize must be rooted in our sign of faith in Christ. Let us demonstrate our faith in God as we walk with Jesus, our brother, friend and Lord.

Sunday Week III (C)

Readings: Exodus 3:1-8, 13-15;
1 Corinthians 10:1-6, 10-12; Luke 13:1-9

God Never Gives Up on Us

The name Robert Stroud is not commonly known. Yet this man's name and his contribution to humanity will live on in the minds of many under a different title, the Birdman of Alcatraz. Robert Stroud was not what one would call an agreeable man. As a teen he was always getting into trouble, starting fights, arguments and squabbles. When he was only nineteen he killed a man in a barroom brawl. Stroud was convicted of second degree murder. Because the crime had occurred on federal property, he was sent to the Federal Penitentiary at Leavenworth, Kansas to serve his sentence.

One might think that being in such a horrible environment as a federal prison would have led Robert Stroud to reform, to get his life in order. Stroud, however, continued his former ways, being even more disruptive and troublesome. One day in the prison a fight broke out among the inmates. Several guards got into the fray to restore order. In the process Stroud stabbed one of the guards with a little wooden knife he had crafted in his cell. The guard died from the attack. The warden at Leavenworth thought the crime was so vicious that he pressed for the death penalty, and the jury agreed. Robert Stroud was scheduled to be executed in the electric chair.

Although it seemed his fate was sealed, God had a plan for Robert Stroud. The plan meant that he should live, and thus an intercessor arose in the form of Stroud's mother. Like any loving parent Mrs. Stroud did not want to see her son die, especially in such an ignoble way as the electric chair. The only person who could commute Stroud's sentence was the President of the United States. Thus, Mrs. Stroud journeyed to Washington, D.C. to see President Woodrow Wilson. Mrs. Stroud was not able to see President Wilson, but she did see the First Lady, who spoke to her husband on Stroud's behalf. Woodrow Wilson commuted Stroud's sentence to life in prison in solitary confinement. Robert Stroud was thus sentenced to spend the rest of his life without seeing any human beings, except the guard once per week when he was allowed the privilege of a shower. Even his meals were slipped through a special opening in his cell door.

God had a plan for Robert Stroud and had not given up on him. The plan began to manifest itself quite innocently one day when a small bird came and perched on the windowsill of Stroud's cell, which looked out onto the Kansas countryside, Stroud's only contact with the outside world. Over time the bird came back. One bird turned into many birds. Stroud received permission to house these creatures in his small cell. He read voraciously all the material he could obtain on birds and their care, especially diseases to which they were susceptible. Stroud conducted many experiments over several years. His study, research and findings were collected into a book published in 1939 as *Stroud's Digest on the Diseases of Birds.* At the time it was the most comprehensive study ever done on bird diseases and their cures.

Robert Stroud was a troublemaker; he was twice convicted of murder. Yet God never gave up on him. God had a plan for Robert Stroud. In the end the plan was revealed and the mission was successfully completed.

We hear in our readings how God never gave up on the Hebrew people, pursuing them at times when they didn't seem to care and even when they rejected him. In bondage in Egypt the Hebrews might have thought God had forgotten them, but such was not the case. God sent Moses to be the great deliverer. We hear today how God revealed himself as "I am who am." God was saying "I am the one who has always been with you and will continue to lead and guide you." As we know from reading the Bible, God was patient with the Hebrews, providing many opportunities to find God and demonstrating infinite compassion when the people repented of their transgressions.

Jesus never gave up on the Jewish people of his day. In the symbolism of the fig tree we hear how the Lord has labored for three years to make the fig tree, namely Israel, bear fruit. The tree is still barren and Jesus wonders if it will ever be productive. But the tree is given another chance. With additional care it may yet produce much fruit. In the same way, God never gave up on the people.

Reconciliation is a powerful theme in Lent and an integral ingredient to our journey home. However, to be reconciled, reunited and healed we need to know that God is ready to welcome us back. We need to accept the fact that God wants us home and will leave no stone unturned in a diligent search to track us down and return us to the fold. The powerful image of Jesus on the cross, with his arms outstretched, invites us to return home. Jesus is waiting to welcome us. He will give us a second, third, a hundredth chance. God never gave up on Robert Stroud and God will never give up on us. Let us open our minds and hearts to the mercy and love of God, which will bring us home to eternal life.

Monday Week III

Readings: 2 Kings 5:1-15; Luke 4:24-30

The Prophetic Challenge

Bartolomé de las Casas came to the New World in 1502 to gain fortune, prestige and independence. He settled on the island of Cuba where he became a successful plantation owner. Hearing a call from God he returned to Europe and was ordained a priest at Rome in 1507. When he returned to Cuba he continued to operate his plantation, which used the native peoples as slaves, a custom unchecked since the time of Columbus. However, through the efforts of people like Father Antonio de Montesinos, who was one of the first to speak out against Spanish cruelty to the natives, las Casas was converted, joined the Dominicans, and dedicated his life to working for the rights of the native American peoples.

As priest and later Bishop of Chiapas (Mexico), las Casas made many attempts to aid the natives, although many Europeans opposed his efforts. He was a prophet who believed that preaching was the key to arousing faith. His words were forceful, in speech and print, but in his day few were listening. His greatest success came in Guatemala in the Vera Paz experiment of 1537-1550. Supported initially by the Spanish king, this plan to convert the natives by peaceful means was successful for several years, but the tension between las Casas, the local settlers and even his fellow Dominicans eventually proved to be too much and the community failed. Las Casas' final prophetic challenge to the methods of Spanish conquest came in a much heralded debate at Valladolid, Spain in 1550 against Juan Genes de Supulveda. Las Casas countered each argument by the learned Supulveda, who used Thomas Aquinas' just war theory to justify hostile action against the natives. Las Casas' efforts challenged the system and many found conversion.

The challenge of the prophetic voice can be experienced in different ways. Naaman, the army commander of the king of Aram, was challenged to believe even when he was not given great signs. He expected that the prophet would do something spectacular in order to cure him. The simplicity of Elisha's request disappointed the Aramean; he wanted to see more. Because he thought that great actions and signs must accompany powerful experiences, he was unwilling to do what was asked. Naaman's challenge was to believe that not only the grandiose and spectacular but ordinary actions can bring renewal and healing.

The Jewish people in Jesus' day also wanted to see a great sign; not all could not accept Christ as the presence of God. Jesus challenged them to recognize and acknowledge their inability to believe, as had happened with earlier generations. But the people were stiff-necked and they did not like to be challenged in this way. Their anger, disappointment and frustration so filled them with indignation that they wanted to kill Jesus.

The prophetic voice still speaks today and it challenges us in many ways, some of which are subtle and others which are more obvious. As Bartolomé de las Casas challenged both the Spanish settlers and his Dominican brothers to find a different, more peaceful way of dealing with the native population, so we are challenged to look inside our hearts and ask how we treat others. Some more dominant prophetic voices speak out on television, radio and in the printed media. However, the prophetic voice of Mother Teresa, who speaks to our sensibilities and priorities by her simplicity, or the humble person of prayer, who by her mere presence invites us to reflect on what is truly important in our lives, challenges us more. The prophetic voice always speaks but often we turn aside because, as our readings describe, we expect something different. Let us be open to the challenge which comes to us in the subtle and the magnificent; may we meet the prophetic challenge this day!

Tuesday Week III

Readings: Daniel 3:25, 34-43; Matthew 18:21-35

The Inner Search for Reconciliation

Oscar Wilde's novel, *The Picture of Dorian Gray,* written in the early part of this century, describes the life of a man who is unable to look honestly at his life. Dorian is a handsome young man who possesses power, wealth and prestige, the three great assets and temptations of contemporary life. An artist, Basil Hallward, who is impressed at Dorian's presence, paints a portrait of him. The portrait is a master work which magically displays the true Dorian who lives inside the physical body—one who is anything but beautiful and handsome. Dorian uses his power to take advantage of others, his wealth to undercut people, and his prestige to position himself where he could do good but always seems to act only for himself. The exterior facade of a handsome and well-groomed man masks the growing ugliness which he carries inside.

One day Dorian observes his portrait and notes how it has changed. The eyes and face look different. They show a sinister, evil man. Dorian locks the picture in his attic, but the image haunts him. In a fit of rage he kills the artist, Basil Hallward, which makes the portrait grow even uglier. In the end Dorian Gray cannot live with himself. His outside good looks remain while inside his corruption grows. The portrait shows the true person—the one that only Dorian knows.

Oscar Wilde's story is a negative example which illustrates an important point. Periodically we need to take the difficult but necessary journey of introspection in order to honestly see who we are and thus, how we usually appear to others. The readings tell us of our need to trust in God, take the inner journey, and change our lives to conform better to what God asks of us. In order to take the inner journey and look at ourselves honestly we must know that God sustains us along the way. Such a task can be perilous, which is perhaps why Dorian Gray never attempted it. God is with us, however, as shown by Azariah's prayer while an exile in Babylon. He asks God to remember the covenant that was made with Abraham, Isaac and Jacob. He prays that God will receive his prayer offering as if it were a large animal holocaust. Azariah is confident that God is with the people and will deal with them mercifully and with great kindness.

In the Gospel we hear of one who cannot look inside and thus finds no reason to forgive, like the story of Dorian Gray. The servant received mercy from the master but has never taken the inner journey to honestly look at his life. Thus he cannot see the ugliness that his life depicts to others. But his fellow servants see him for his true self and report him to the master, being badly shaken about the incident. When the master summons the servant the day of reckoning comes, just as Dorian Gray stood before the portrait and saw his true self. The picture of the servant reflects his malice and he receives a severe punishment for his failure to look inside.

During Lent we must look into our hearts and souls and see what they truly hold. Honesty is absolutely necessary in this, for God knows all there is. We can't disguise our actions or run from who we are. If we cannot look inside then we will never know what needs to be corrected and how to move along in our road home to God. Azariah's confidence in God must be our attitude as well. With the knowledge that God is always with us, forgives any transgressions, and guides us to a better way of life, we can avoid the failures of Dorian Gray and the servant in the Gospel. Let us, with trust and hope, take the inner journey, discover our need for God's forgiveness, and then continue our walk toward our home with God and eternal life.

Wednesday Week III

Readings: Deuteronomy 4:1, 5-9; Matthew 5:17-19

The Law of Freedom

Many people find politics a highly attractive game. People play it on the campaign trails, in smoked-filled conference rooms, and on the floors of legislatures. Most of us, however, play this most important game as armchair quarterbacks from the security of our homes as we watch the evening news after a tough day at the office. In the game of politics we use the law like a baseball to batter people around, manipulate them and at times even destroy them in the contest. The game is played in ways which cover a wide spectrum of opinion. On one side are people we might call Jeffersonians, who believe in a government that governs best when it governs least. On the other side are those who believe, as did the proponents of the New Deal in the 1930s, that government has a responsibility to assure that certain services and programs are in place for its citizens. Between these two "bookends" the game is played, many times weighing the letter of the law against its spirit.

The Jewish people were not only devoted to the law; it was the foundation of their whole way of life. As the author of Deuteronomy says, God gave the people the law so that they would have a code to live by. They were told to observe it closely so it would be a sign to others of the Hebrews' wisdom and intelligence. The law was given, however, not just to impress the people and their neighbors, but to provide a framework of life, a way to live and be free. A great nation is one which has laws and decrees that are just and which draw people to live in greater harmony with one another and with other countries.

The importance of the law was certainly not lost on Jesus. As he says in today's Gospel, "Do not think that I have come to abolish the law or the prophets; I have come not to abolish but to fulfill" (Mt 5:17). The Lord goes on to say that those who ignore the law will be least in God's kingdom while those who fulfill God's commands will be great in heaven. Jesus' words might have been confusing to his listeners since at times he did not abide by the technical precepts of Mosaic practice, such as strict Sabbath observance. But we need to understand what Jesus means by fulfillment of the law. The law is two-fold—it has its letter or technical side and its spirit or reason side. Jesus came to show us how to apply the spirit of the law to our lives, to enrich them and in the process to draw closer to God. The Lord's words indicate that the spirit of the law is vital, for it is this understanding which fulfills and completes what God intended in giving the law to Moses.

Many political discussions and even arguments are fought over the relative importance of the letter and the spirit of the law. God gave us the concept of law to make us free so that we might choose God over the world. God never intended to place human beings in straight jackets and demand compliance with the law. Rather God gave us free will, intelligence and the opportunity for education to make wise decisions. The law was instituted for us; we were not made for the law. If lived properly and fully the law sets us free and gives us all sorts of opportunities, but if we restrict the purpose of the law to either its letter or spirit, then we limit our options and our freedom as well. Let us enjoy and live both the letter and spirit of the law. It will help us to know the truth and the truth will set us free.

Thursday Week III

Readings: Jeremiah 7:23-28; Luke 11:14-23

Never Counting the Cost

People perform heroic acts for others and often do them without counting the cost. Each year on the island of Oahu in Hawaii the "iron man" competition tests the endurance, strength and perseverance of athletes from around the world. Men and women compete together in a grueling all day athletic competition of ocean swimming, bike riding and running. Several years ago one man entered the competition with his son, but not in the manner officials expected. The man's son was crippled, but that did not deter the father from bringing his boy with him. In the first event, a torturous two and a half mile swim in the ocean, the boy was tied to a raft which the father towed behind him as he swam. Next, during the 125 mile bicycle race over the lava highways of the island, the boy rode in a basket on the handle bars of the bike. Finally after these two grueling events the father tackled the last event—the marathon—a twenty-six mile foot race. His son still went along, this time strapped to his father's back. At the end of the competition reporters from around the world gathered around the man and his son, amazed at what they had witnessed. They asked him, "Why did you do it?" He simply answered, "I did it for my son because he will never be able to do it." The father performed a heroic feat without counting the cost.

Maximilian Kolbe, a Polish Franciscan priest and writer, performed a heroic act that has since captured the attention of the world. During World War II, Kolbe, like many clerics and ministers, was incarcerated by the Nazis. One day at the Auschwitz concentration camp a prisoner escaped. Angered, the commandant wanted to teach the prisoners a lesson. He ordered ten men to be executed for the one who had escaped. Guards randomly selected ten candidates who were paraded in front of the assembled inmates and camp guards. Kolbe, who witnessed this scene, knew that one of the men selected had a wife and family. The priest offered to die in that man's place. Maximilian Kolbe's courage and martyrdom led to his canonization by Pope John Paul II.

Jeremiah lived a heroic life without counting the cost. He had been sent by God to proclaim the Lord's message to the nation of Judah. God was giving the Hebrews another chance to reform, to get their lives in order, and to continue their practice of the Mosaic law. I am sure that Jeremiah was disappointed and he longed for a task that might be fulfilling and less arduous. But such was not to be his lot—the Hebrews would not listen; faithfulness had disappeared from the land. Despite the difficulty of his work, Jeremiah, like the athletic father and St. Maximilian, did not count the cost. He did what God asked of him and refused to bend to pressure, discouraging results, or rejection by others. Although many proved unfaithful, Jeremiah would remain faithful to the end.

Sent by the Father on a mission to establish the reign of God on earth, Jesus never counted the cost in his work. Not only did many not believe in him or appreciate his message, some even placed him in league with Satan, as today's Gospel recounts. When Jesus did not perform or produce as others thought he should, they rejected his message. But like his predecessor Jeremiah, Jesus did not count the cost and never flinched from his mission, even when others turned against him. Jesus continued his mission, even to shedding his blood so that we might find life.

As Christians we have been called to lead lives of holiness and discipleship. Our challenges will probably not be as dramatic as that of the heroic father, Maximilian Kolbe or Jeremiah. But in subtle and at times great ways we will find our beliefs, values and purpose in life challenged. How will we respond? The tendency today is to go with the flow, because it is easier and more convenient, even when it might not be what we know is right. May the challenge in today's Scriptures, as well as the example of the father and St. Maximilian, strengthen our resolve to never count the cost, even if it be our own lives. Let us live our common vocation to holiness; let us live for God and never count the cost.

Friday Week III

Readings: Hosea 14:2-10; Mark 12:28-34

Taking the Road Home

Most people enjoy the opportunity to travel. Whether it is for work, education or pleasure, travel offers new and different opportunities which we anticipate with a sense of joy, adventure and wonder. All who travel, from the experienced person to the novice, must plan the trip in order to achieve its purpose. First, we need to know where we are going. Most of the time this is the easiest part of the planning, for our purpose—work, visit or some other activity—determines our destination. We cannot make plans without knowing where we are going. Next we must plan how to get to our destination. Not only must we determine the mode of our trip—plane, train, automobile or even foot—but we must decide the route to be used. Some people prefer a direct path which allows them to get to their final destination as quickly as possible, while others will use a more scenic route. Still others, due to construction on the road or a need to see others along the way, may choose a circuitous route. Before taking our trip we must also ask ourselves what we hope to accomplish. What is the reason for our travel; what is our goal?

The season of Lent is a journey that eventually leads home to God. In some ways we have been forced onto this road by how the Church determines the liturgical calendar. But because God gives us free will we can always decide to accept or reject the various opportunities which are provided. Thus, we have consciously taken this road in an attempt to grow closer to the Lord, our lasting peace and final home. As we approach the midpoint in our journey we hear readings that speak to us about our trip, why we travel, how we can best do it, and what our goals should be.

The prophet Hosea, who prophesied to the Northern Kingdom of Israel, knew that the people needed to get on the road and return to God. His words are crystal clear, "Return, O Israel, to the Lord, your God" (Hos 14:1). Hosea suggests that the Hebrews must travel to God to seek forgiveness for their lack of faithfulness and to render to God some offering of their goodness. The goal of our journey is, of course, to find God's forgiveness, to become reconciled with the Creator. The prophet says that the wise and prudent person will understand the need for this journey, enter upon it and prosper.

The path we must take is not easy but is succinctly given us by Jesus in the Gospel. The Golden Rule, love of God and love of neighbor, appears to be a simple path because of its brevity, but we all know how great a challenge it is to love God and our brothers and sisters. Life gives us plenty of bumps and bruises; we are knocked down, pushed off the road, and even turned in the opposite direction from the path which we seek. But the true Christian is one who does his or her best to brush off the dust of the road, bind the wounds that life inflicts, and with a future vision retake the highway and continue the journey home to God. To love God and our neighbor requires our best effort.

During Lent we can spend extra time examining our life to check why we are on the road, what path we have chosen, and most importantly, what is our goal. Let us keep our perspective clear in what we do and why we do it. Let us continue on the road to Easter and to eternal life.

Saturday Week III

Readings: Hosea 6:1-6; Luke 18:9-14

The Attitude of Sincerity

A man had a dream in which he found himself in heaven. He was walking along and came upon Jesus, who allowed him a vision of what was happening on earth. In the vision the man saw a church on Sunday morning where Mass was in progress. The organist appeared to be playing, since her fingers were moving up and down the keyboard and her feet were pushing the pedals—but the man could not hear a sound. He also saw what appeared to be the congregation singing, but he could not hear them. He watched the priest and the people as the Mass progressed. From all his years as a Catholic he knew exactly what was going on and what he should be hearing—but no sound was audible. The man was quite puzzled by the vision so he turned to the Lord and asked why there was silence when he could see all that was happening. Jesus replied, "Unless people pray or sing from their hearts, we cannot hear them."

This story speaks clearly of the need to be sincere in what we do and say. What we do means little, but how and why we do it means everything. The attitude we take in the experiences of our daily lives is all important.

God's words pronounced by Hosea tell us how important attitude is in our approach to God. The people of Ephraim and Judah brought their prayer and offering to God with a shallowness that was easily detected. Their plea to God was empty, like a morning cloud of dew which passes away so early. God was disappointed in their lack of sincerity. They professed by their actions that the way to God was by great feats and daring acts. But God wants sincerity expressed in love and knowledge of God rather than sacrifice or holocaust.

The Gospel presents the classic contrast between people who act so as to be noticed and those who realize that God desires an attitude of true humility. The Pharisee is egocentric; he thinks only of himself and how his prayer and actions will be observed by his peers. God plays no role in his actions. The tax collector, on the other hand, realizes that he not only needs God, but that without God he is nothing. He knows that he is imperfect and does not try to impress others with his life. Jesus' analysis of the situation is succinct and clear, "All who exalt themselves will be humbled, but all who humble themselves will be exalted" (Lk 18:14).

One of the challenges of life today is to accomplish great things for God without exalting ourselves. For the Christian, a good perspective on this dilemma can be kept by always asking oneself, "What is the attitude I take in my daily tasks?" If our work is an act of the head alone then no commitment exists, and thus our efforts will be shallow and take us off track. But if we are guided by our hearts then our daily tasks move to a higher level where we point toward God's kingdom as the reason for our labors.

Sincerity in heart and attitude transforms an ordinary task into something special; it becomes God's work and helps establish the reign of God in our midst. Let us think about *why* and *how* we do things and focus less on *what* we do. Sincerity of heart is a prayer heard in heaven!

Meditations for the Fourth Week of Lent

Sunday Week IV (A)

Readings: 1 Samuel 16:1, 6-7, 10-13;
Ephesians 5:8-14; John 9:1-41

Seek the Light of Christ

Anne Sullivan was a true miracle worker. As a special teacher of the deaf and blind, Anne's gifts enabled her to reach out and touch others. She brought light to the darkness which pervaded the lives of many handicapped people. But in 1885 Anne Sullivan met the challenge of her life when she was introduced to a young girl who was deaf, dumb and blind, Helen Keller. Anne came to teach, to befriend and to love Helen, but she faced high barriers. Helen Keller was a child who was fearfully alone, cut off from the world in total silence and darkness.

Anne Sullivan's initial challenge was not to teach Helen, but to find a way to enter her world. She could not cure the child's blindness nor deafness, which were physical realities. Yet she could search for ways to cure a darker blindness, a more silent deafness which plagued Helen Keller. Helen was a victim of neglect; nobody seemed to care. No one recognized the beauty and potential which existed inside her.

To meet this demanding task, Anne first had to gain Helen's confidence. Anne needed to instill in Helen the knowledge that someone could break through the silence and the darkness. Ultimately Anne gained Helen's confidence.

Although everyone had thought Helen was incapable of learning, she was found to be quite intelligent. She first learned to read Braille. Then she learned to talk—first words, then sentences and finally conversations.

Anne Sullivan brought the light of recognition to a person whom others had discarded as a loss to society. Through many years of work Helen Keller was prepared for college. She entered Radcliffe at the age of sixteen, two years earlier than most of her contemporaries who enjoyed full health. Over her lifetime Helen Keller became world famous as a symbol for those with disabilities. But it was Anne Sullivan, the miracle worker, who brought the light and recognized the goodness that existed in Helen and all people.

Our readings today speak about recognizing the light of God's presence in our world. In the first reading Jesse is amazed that God has not chosen one of his elder sons to be the next king. Like many of us, Jesse expects that the powerful and strong will be singled out. He does not even think of presenting his young son David to Samuel. Jesse is somewhat blind. Samuel opens his eyes and cures his spiritual blindness by anointing David.

In the Gospel we hear the familiar story of Jesus' cure of the man born blind. Jesus commands him, "Go wash in the pool of Siloam" (Jn 9:7). The man goes and is cured of his physical blindness. But the Lord does much more for him. The man has not only been physically blind from birth, he has been spiritually blind as well; he has not believed. Jesus gives the man the opportunity he needs, allowing him to recognize the presence of God. Jesus asks, "Do you believe in the Son of Man?" The man is obviously hungry to believe. He responds, "And who is he, sir? Tell me, so that I may believe in him." When Jesus reveals his identity the man confirms his faith, "Lord, I believe!" (Jn 9:35-38). With this statement of faith and commitment the man's sight is fully restored.

The man cured by Jesus is contrasted with the Pharisees who can physically see, but are blind to more important things. The Pharisees accuse Jesus of being a sinner. They are spiritually blind to God's presence but this condition is self-imposed; they were not born this way. They have purposely shut out the light. Remember Jesus says, "I am the light of the world" (Jn 9:5). Jesus has come to open the eyes of the spiritually blind, but judgment is passed on those who refuse to recognize him.

During the season of Lent we undergo many trials, as Jesus did in the desert. The things of this world tempt us. Jesus challenges us to transform our lives and to find the living water of his love. Today we are asked to shake off the blindness that sometimes comes; we are asked to seek the light. In our second reading St. Paul urges us to seek the light and avoid the darkness. Light produces goodness, justice and truth. Darkness shuts out God, but Christ brings the light which no darkness can overcome. We must be receptive to the light.

How well do we see, not physically but spiritually? How well do we recognize the presence of God; how well do we see the light? Like a burning candle, the light of Christ spreads out in all directions evenly, without discrimination. If we cannot see the light it is because we do not want to see or we hide from it. Sometimes we may be like the Pharisees who intentionally shut out the light.

The light of the world is here; it is all around us. But how difficult at times it is to see and recognize its presence. Let us seek the light and throw off darkness as Anne Sullivan helped Helen Keller to do. Let us radiate to all God's people the goodness, justice and truth that the light bestows.

Sunday Week IV (B)

Readings: 2 Chronicles 36:14-17, 19-23; Ephesians 2:4-10; John 3:14-21

The Light of the World

Scientists tells us that if you take six molecules of carbon dioxide, combine it with twelve molecules of water, and then add light, the result will be one molecule of glucose, six molecules of oxygen, and six molecules of water. This process, known as photosynthesis, makes the world as we know it possible. Carbon dioxide, which is exhaled by all mammals, is converted into oxygen which allows us to breathe. Plants make life on earth possible by carrying out photosynthesis. But this chemical reaction cannot occur without light.

Light is an essential element in our lives. It warms our earth and our feelings as well. We feel more comfortable in the light. Darkness is cold; it brings fear and danger. Light also gives us strength. We feel more confident when we walk in the light. Light strengthens our will and gives us direction. We can go forward when we walk in the light since we know which way to go. Light illumines our path, the road of our daily journey as well as that of our life.

Our readings today describe the light which gives direction to our lives. The light will always come to us, but we may or may not follow. This choice is our free will.

We have the existential choice of saying yes or no to God. In the reading from Second Chronicles we hear that the light came to the Hebrew people, but it was rejected. The light came in the form of the prophets. They came to show the chosen people of God the way and to give warmth and strength by their words of encouragement. They came to give direction by the word of God which they proclaimed. But as the author of Chronicles tells us, the people mocked God's messengers. They scoffed at the prophets and despised the warnings which they gave. Thus, God punished the Hebrews with exile to Babylon. Still, even with their refusal to follow the light, God never gave up on them. The light was sent again, this time to Cyrus, the king of Persia. The light was sent to tell Cyrus that the people should be returned to Israel.

In the Gospel we again hear about the light. John says the light came into the world, not to condemn it but to save it. Unfortunately, some people of Jesus' day, like their ancestors, did not pay attention to the light. As with the prophets, Jesus came to give warmth, to renew strength, and to give hope. Jesus came to give direction to a world which was moving toward ruin. Despite all the possibilities that Jesus provided, John says that the people preferred darkness. The light exposed their wicked deeds. The people rejected the light and chose the darkness instead. They lost their direction and found themselves in coldness and despair.

Photosynthesis enables the natural world to keep on going. But the light which is Jesus gives direction, meaning and sustenance to the world. Sunlight brings warmth, strength, and direction. It is essential for our physical well being. Similarly, we cannot survive spiritually without the light of Christ! As St. Paul says to the Ephesians, through Christ we have been brought back to life from the darkness of sin. Through the light of Christ salvation is ours through faith. We need Jesus, his warmth, strength, comfort and direction. Through our ability to choose, we can say yes or no to God. But Jesus says that those who say no are condemned. We must say yes to God; we must seek the light. Whoever welcomes the light avoids condemnation and finds eternal life.

Each day is an opportunity to rediscover the light. As the Gospel says, "For God so loved the world that he gave his only Son, so that everyone who believes in him may not perish but may have eternal life" (Jn 3:16). God sent the Son, the light, so that we could return to the Father. Let us seek the light and welcome the Lord. Let us say yes to God's call in our life and in this way find eternal salvation as well.

Sunday Week IV (C)

Readings: Joshua 5:9-12;
2 Corinthians 5:17-21; Luke 15:1-3, 11-32

The Journey of Reconciliation

Joseph Girzone, in his book *Joshua and the Children,* the second in a series of books which center about a contemporary Christ figure named Joshua, tells the following story. About 100 years ago in France a butler worked for a wealthy Parisian family. This butler excelled at his work, but he was also quite greedy. He had worked for the family for many years but he felt that his services were not appreciated and that he was not paid sufficiently. Actually he was paid better than most domestic servants in Paris. The butler in his greed plotted to steal the family fortune which he had discovered was locked in a vault below the house. He realized, however, that in order to steal the fortune and escape there could be no witnesses. Thus he decided to eliminate the whole family to make sure no one would know.

One night very late the butler entered the house. It was easy to enter, for as the butler he had a house key. He first went to the bedroom of the parents and while they slept he quietly murdered both of them. He then continued, going from bedroom to bedroom, to eliminate each child. In the process some commotion aroused the youngest child, a boy of seven years. Somehow he realized what was happening, and although terrified, kept his head and crept out of his bedroom into a hall closet where he hid under some old clothes. The butler never found him, but made off with the family fortune nonetheless.

The little boy was so frightened that he fled the house before the authorities discovered the horrible scene. He walked the streets, choosing to remain homeless. Many years later he entered a church for sanctuary and asked the pastor for permission to stay. He was admitted to the little community and over time entered the seminary and was ordained a priest. For a few years after his ordination the new priest served in Parisian parishes. After some time he was assigned by the government to be a chaplain at the infamous French prison on Devil's Island.

One day while he was on duty at the prison an inmate and an accompanying guard came to him. "Come quickly, Father," they said, "a prisoner in the field is dying." The chaplain, who was always ready, grabbed his little satchel and ran off with the two men. When they arrived the priest knelt down over an older man who was breathing heavily. "Do you want to confess your sins?" he asked. He received no response. Again he asked, "May I hear your confession?" The man shook his head no. "Why not?" pleaded the priest. "Because God could never forgive me for what I have done," the man gasped.

After a few minutes the chaplain managed to convince the inmate to tell his story. Many years ago he was working as a butler for a wealthy Parisian family. He was greedy and had stolen the family fortune. In the process he had murdered the whole family except the youngest boy who had escaped. He was tortured inside over what he had done. When the prisoner ended his story the priest looked at him with love and said, "If I can forgive you then God can certainly forgive you. It was my family that you murdered and I am that little boy. I forgive you from my heart." The prisoner broke down in tears as did the priest. As absolution was given the prisoner died.

This powerful story speaks of the total love and forgiveness of one human being for another. Our readings speak of forgiveness and love, the unbounded and unlimited love and forgiveness of God, a love without reservation. We might call it a story of the journey of reconciliation.

The Gospel story is familiar to all of us. Most people call this text the parable of the prodigal son. But depending on how one reads it, the story could also be rightly labeled the parable of the forgiving father or the parable of the unforgiving son. Like the priest-chaplain, the father in the story, who represents God, shows total love and forgiveness for his wayward, so-called prodigal son. Forgiveness is complete; the past is forgotten. The Book of Joshua tells us how God removed the reproach from Israel; just so the father removes the reproach from his son. Reconciliation calls for celebration. For the Hebrews it meant eating the fruit of the new land, the land of milk and honey. For the prodigal son it meant eating the fatted calf. God welcomes back the sinner with no questions asked.

The forgiveness of the father is actually the last step in a longer process or journey of reconciliation. The process begins with ourselves. We should notice in the Gospel parable that reconciliation was initiated when the younger son realized he was in a predicament. He began to see that he needed others and internally he made the vital first step to return in thought to his home. This is the first critical step in the journey. We must also note that the father spotted his son at a distance and ran to him. Not one word was spoken and still reconciliation occurred.

Once the important first step in the journey of reconciliation has been completed then the second step must be taken—reconciliation with others. In the Gospel we receive a negative example of this process. The older son is an angry man. He cannot forgive his brother and he cannot understand his father. This son would not have understood what St. Paul tells us in the second reading. Paul says that since God has forgiven us all our transgressions, we must forgive the faults of others. He goes on to say that we have been entrusted with the message of reconciliation. We are to be ambassadors of Christ's love and forgiveness to others. This is a great responsibility. The elder brother's inability to love and show forgiveness to others breaks the chain in the process; reconciliation is stunted.

Life is a journey, with a beginning, a middle and an end. Birth is our beginning in this world, the middle is our day-to-day life, and death, when we return to the one from whom we came, is the end. The journey of life has many sub-journeys, each with a beginning, a middle, and an end. There is the journey of our education and the journey of relationship, which for many is marriage. There is the journey of our professional work.

Lent is a journey as well. It has a beginning, Ash Wednesday, and it has an end, the Easter Triduum. The vast middle is the season we now celebrate. During this season, this journey of faith, we are asked to spend some time reflecting on our need to make the journey of reconciliation in our lives. The trip begins with ourselves; the inner path must be searched. What do we find and can we accept it? What is right and what is not so right? What needs correction? The Christian today demonstrates his or her greatest prowess, not in power, wealth and prestige, the three great temptations of our society, but rather in one's ability to acknowledge weakness and brokenness, and the need for personal healing and reconciliation. Once we have done this, then we must move to our fellow travelers, the other pilgrims on the road and find reconciliation with them—family, friends, colleagues and perhaps one with whom we have some great difficulty. Lastly, we find reconciliation with our God, the one whose love for us is beyond anything we can imagine.

The prisoner found reconciliation when he admitted his guilt. The prodigal son found conversion when he realized his need for others. As our Lenten journey continues, may we ponder our need for reconciliation. Let us accept and forgive ourselves; let us then be ambassadors of Christ's love to others. May we accept the loving embrace of Jesus this day!

Monday Week IV

Readings: Isaiah 65:17-21; John 4:43-54

God Recreates the World

For many people spring is the most delightful season of the year. After a winter where snow and bitter cold may have dominated the weather, spring comes to refresh us, provide new beginnings, and change our perspective on almost everything. Spring is the world's annual re-creation when the bulbs and flowers shoot forth in all their splendor, trees bud blossoms and new leaves, and the sun warms the earth, inviting us to break out of our lethargy and begin anew. The world needs its springtime. It is a time to start over, try new things, experience new opportunities. It is a season given by God for the world to prepare itself for the opportunities that the dynamism of nature provides.

The Church gives us Lent to prepare ourselves for the Easter Triduum, the most solemn and important time in the liturgical cycle. We cannot experience the Easter alleluia nor the joy and beauty present in the Easter lily unless we have adequately prepared ourselves for these special events. We need to be created anew in mind, heart and spirit to fully enter into the Paschal mystery and its powerful message.

In our readings today we hear how God recreates people's lives. The Hebrews experienced the pain and suffering of exile while in Babylon for fifty years. The prophets had foretold that the people would be punished for their failure to reform and abide by the covenant and Mosaic law. But as we know from the Scriptures, they disregarded the message, disappointed God, and found themselves subjected to a foreign power. Upon their return to Israel Isaiah speaks to the people of how God will recreate their world and give them a fresh start. God will create new heavens and a new earth; the things of the past will be forgotten. God will give new birth to the people, physically by returning them to the land, but more importantly in their hearts and minds by recreating an environment of rejoicing and happiness. They will live secure in their homes and eat of the produce of the land.

In the Gospel Jesus brings new life to the son of the royal official. We are given little information about this man but we know that he possessed faith. He heard that Jesus had returned to Galilee and he went to him for help. Probably news of Jesus' miracles and signs spread by word of mouth. The royal official placed his trust in the Lord's words that his son would live; he believed that Christ could bring new life. Jesus rewarded the official's faith and healed the boy without even seeing him.

Re-creation is an idea which we must strive to attain each day. The Father continually gives us opportunities to discover new ways to serve God and others. God's recreative force, however, is not thrust upon us without our choice. God places opportunity and possibility before us, but we must have the confidence, trust and faith necessary to utilize God's gifts to make a difference in our lives. Many opportunities for renewal will come our way this Lenten season as we travel the road that leads to God. Let us open our hearts and minds, as well as our eyes and ears to these possibilities of renewal. Trust and confidence in God, lived in the spirit of Lent will create us anew, prepare us for the Easter mysteries, and lead us closer to eternal life.

Tuesday Week IV

Readings: Ezekiel 47:1-9, 12; John 5:1-3, 5-16

Jesus Is Our Living Water

Although it is a rather simple chemical compound and often taken for granted, water is one of the world's most valuable natural resources. Ancient civilizations knew its importance and built their great cities along a major river, sea, lake or ocean. Water served as a means of transportation, for pleasure and commerce, but its applications grew over time. Through experimentation or coincidence it was learned that water was the basic component of many different compounds. The Greeks believed all things to be some combination of earth, air, fire and water. Water was used to nourish people, animals and plants; life could not exist without it. Water was found to be a nearly universal solvent, the primary agent for cleansing, and it became a symbol of purity in religious celebration. Although human civilization aspired to many things, it couldn't survive without water.

Today's readings describe water's symbolism and the source of its power. Ezekiel speaks of water's capacity to bring life. The great river which he must swim across is the source of life for every sort of living thing. Additionally, the water in the river is powerful in its ability to transform the sea into fresh water. Along the banks of the river all sorts of fruit trees grow which bear fruit each month. The fruit of the tree serves as food and its leaves as medicine.

The Temple is the source of the water which Ezekiel describes. It comes from God who gives the water its strength, power and ability to nourish. As the source of sustenance for all that brings life, God's power is much stronger than water. God shows the prophet that without God as its source, water is useless.

In Jerusalem the sheep pool of Bethesda was famous as a place where the sick could find healing. The action of the water drew many to this place in hopes of being cured, including the man whom Jesus encounters. From the story it appears that the man placed his whole trust in the power of the water. He probably had read or heard the Scriptures, like Ezekiel, and thus knew the power of water. Seeing others being healed at Bethesda confirmed his belief. But Jesus wants the man to know that ultimately the power of God is the source of new life. The water is only an instrument provided by God to bring strength, relief and sustenance to all living things.

Jesus is the source of our strength—he is our living water. Water can only work its miracles because God has chosen it to serve as a special agent of life. In different ways the vitality, strength and life-sustaining purpose of water is lived out in our relationships with one another. Jesus is the living water, but we must, in ways that are given to us, water and nourish those around us. God gives us opportunities each day to bring the life-giving power of water to bear in a situation. Sometimes we have the opportunity to feed someone, whether it be with food and drink, God's word, or a sense of compassion. Other times we can be the power and strength that another needs, defending the rights of the alien, the unborn or those who are persecuted. We can also be the cleansing action of water to others by listening, giving a word of advice, or finding reconciliation.

Jesus, the one who is the water of life, asks us to strengthen, encourage, challenge and feed those who are part of our lives. Our action will only be as good as our connection to the source of life, Jesus. As we continue our journey home, let us align ourselves more closely to God, experience his cleansing and feeding action, and then as renewed children of God, share our lives with others.

Wednesday Week IV

Readings: Isaiah 49:8-15; John 5:17-30

Imitating the Community of God

During the course of the Christian era many fundamental questions have arisen which have provided grist for the mill of theological discussion. Two of the most important and mystifying concepts, which are central to our faith, are the Church and the Trinity. Over the centuries many different answers have been proposed to the question, "What is the Church?" Today, however, as a result of the Second Vatican Council, the view that the Church as the people of God, is most popular and best received. In his book *A Church to Believe In*, Avery Dulles presents the concept of the Church as a community of disciples. Rather than a pyramidal hierarchy of clerics, the Church is understood, using the Pauline model, as the Body of Christ, in which all contribute in important and different ways.

By its nature as an absolute mystery, the Trinity is a more difficult concept to grasp. For centuries great theologians, including Augustine, Thomas Aquinas, and more recently Karl Rahner, have written treatises in attempts to elucidate the Trinity. One thing that seems clear through the complicated discussions of these learned thinkers is that the Trinity, like the Church, is a community. God, as Father, Son and Holy Spirit, acts as Creator, Redeemer and Sanctifier, but always in a unity of one.

The concept of community and the love which acts

as the glue to hold this special union together has been ingrained in the Judeo-Christian understanding of society from the beginning. God called Abraham to gather together a people who would be his offspring; he would be the father of a great nation. Through the time of Moses, the judges, the kings and the prophets, the lived experience of the people forged a belief in Israel as a community. Even when they thought God had abandoned them, as we hear in today's first reading, the fundamental belief that the people must stay together remained strong. However, the people were slow to learn and believe that love must glue their community together, just as God, the ever-faithful one, showed love to them. When the Hebrews were in exile in Babylon, God told them through the words of Isaiah that they would be restored to their land; a highway through the mountains would be constructed. God will not forget his people. As Isaiah says, "Can a woman forget her nursing child, or show no compassion for the child of her womb? Even these may forget, yet I will not forget you" (Is 49:15).

In the Gospel Jesus speaks of the special unity of God which is expressed in love. The Father and Son love each other and through this mutual relationship, together with the Holy Spirit, they guide the world. Jesus speaks of how the Father and Son work together in ways which give life to the world. The community of God which we call the Trinity is bound together in love. This love, shared with the human race, must be our example of how to live.

We are all members of various communities. There is a community in our place of work, another in our neighborhood, and still others in clubs, sports teams and various recreational pursuits. For these communities to function well, a glue must hold them together, allowing the members to draw strength from one another. Love must bind us together. Love would not allow God to abandon the rebellious Hebrew people; love unites the three Persons of the Trinity. In similar ways we must demonstrate our love for one another so as to bind together the various communities in which we participate. When we show love we imitate the God who first loved us. Jesus, the Son, made the supreme sacrifice of love by his death on the cross. In our daily words and actions let us participate in the community of God through an attitude of love. Scripture reports the observations of those who observed the early Christian community, "See how they love one another." May we have the courage to live that same love.

Thursday Week IV

Readings: Exodus 32:7-14; John 5:31-47

Can We Accept God?

In today's society it is almost impossible to get a job without a resumé, or as academic people call it, a *curriculum vitae,* or CV for short. A resumé gives an employer a short summary of our life, describing our education, work experience, special skills and abilities. A resumé succinctly tells another who we are and what qualifications we possess. A good resumé is a must in today's business world. All sorts of books and many different companies exist to help people prepare one. When hundreds or possibly even thousands of people apply for one position, one's resumé must stand out and catch the employer's attention. A good resumé can often pave the way to an interview and possibly a job.

God certainly does not need a resumé, but it is written nevertheless throughout the Scriptures and amounts to a highly impressive record. God demonstrated power in rescuing the Hebrews from bondage in Egypt. Who else could raise up such a leader as Moses, work so many miracles, and stand by the people even when they were disobedient and ungrateful? Today's first reading speaks of God's power to forgive. God realized the people were "stiff-necked." Even when they had witnessed his action on their behalf they continued to turn away. The worship of the molten calf violated the first and basic commandment of God. The people knew better, but they acted out of impatience. God's wrath was directed toward those who had transgressed the law, but Moses interceded for the people. Moses urged God to demonstrate other vital qualities—forgiveness and mercy. Although the people were not worthy of such compassion, God relented in the planned punishment and the Hebrew nation was saved.

In the Gospel Jesus speaks of the various references that would be listed in his resumé. John the Baptist was one of the first to testify on Jesus' behalf. People listened to what John said. For a short while he was a lamp set aflame and burning brightly. But their interest faded quickly; it seems that the one for whom John spoke mattered little to them. Jesus has additional personal references. God the Father gives testimony on Jesus' behalf. Again, however, the people have chosen not to accept this personal reference. Lastly, Jesus says that the Scriptures themselves testify to his life and purpose, but others are unwilling to come and find life in God. Jesus has come, not of his own accord, but to fulfill the will of God. But the people continue in their obstinacy and refuse to believe.

The credentials which God displayed to the Hebrew people have been made more clear and are better defined today than ever before, but society continues to reject them. In almost every aspect of human existence great strides have been made since the time of Jesus. We have made the world a smaller place by our mastery of the means of transportation and communication. We have reduced human suffering and extended life expectancy greatly through advances in medicine. Technologically it is possible to buy all that you need, learn what you want, and entertain yourself without leaving the privacy and comfort of your own home. We have come so far, all with God's help, but have we made any real strides in accepting God? God's CV is quite impressive; his mighty works, tremendous power and personal references are beyond compare, yet often we refuse to give God the job. We choose other things and people to provide what we need or want. Like the stubborn Hebrews we refuse to accept the immediate presence of God.

Lent is a time for us to take stock of our spiritual lives. Along this journey which leads home we will find obstacles, ruts, detours and roadblocks. God's qualifications as the one who can help us overcome these difficulties and return to the correct road are impeccable. God is present, possesses a complete resumé, and is willing to help. Let us accept God this day!

Friday Week IV

Readings: Wisdom 2:1, 12-22;
John 7:1-2, 10, 25-30

The Challenge of Righteousness

Daniel Rutiger, "Rudy" to his friends, dreamed about playing football for the University of Notre Dame. He shared his dream with his family, classmates and teammates at Joliet Catholic High School, and his co-workers at the local steel mill where he worked. Everyone told him it was foolish to pursue such a quest—Notre Dame, they said, is for rich kids, bright students and great athletes—not for an ordinary guy like Rudy. Others' lack of confidence, however, did not deter him from his goal. Circumstances tested his will and stamina but eventually Rudy's dream began to unfold. He went to South Bend, Indiana and enrolled at Holy Cross College, across the street from Notre Dame. He studied hard, made many friends, and found contacts with the groundskeepers who maintained the field at Notre Dame stadium.

Two years after his arrival in South Bend, Rudy was accepted at the university. He was successful as a "walk-on" and became a member of the practice squad for the Fighting Irish. Rudy was small and did not possess great athletic ability, but he did have the heart of a lion. His determination attracted the attention of the coaches and his teammates. Some of the team's starters, however, felt that Rudy was working too hard, making them look bad in practice. Coaches chided the scholarship athletes to play as well as Rudy. His teammates told him to slow down—who was he trying to impress? Sometimes their anger at him exploded into sharp words, but they usually vented it on the practice field where Rudy was a marked man.

Over time Rudy's perseverance and courage won the day. His teammates began to respect him and spoke highly of him to the coaches. Rudy was not a great football player, but he did challenge others to strive harder and make the most of their opportunities.

Rudy's experience of rejection by his teammates for doing what was right illustrates the message in today's Scripture readings. The author of the Book of Wisdom speaks in prophetic terms of Jesus' rejection by his own people. Jesus is the "just one" who is viewed as obnoxious because he challenges people with transgressions of the law and violations of their earlier training. The author speaks of how the just one will be rejected—merely to see him will be a hardship. The people plan to test the validity of the just one's words. The test will begin with revilement and torture and it will end with a shameful death.

We have reached a critical point in our Lenten journey, as today's readings indicate. For the first time the reality of Jesus' passion and death are foretold. In the Gospel we hear that some are plotting Jesus' death. The Lord can only go to Jerusalem to celebrate the Feast of Booths in secret, for his enemies are looking for an opportunity to kill him. Like Rudy, Jesus is not afraid of those who reject him, but he challenges them at every step in their lack of belief. The crowds are unable to apprehend him, however, since his hour has not yet come.

The goal of our Lenten journey is rapidly approaching, but we still have much to do. Our readings today ask us to think how we may have rejected someone simply because that person has challenged us to do more, think bigger, or strive harder. No one is happy when others make us appear lazy or slack in our efforts. Yet, if someone else is doing his or her utmost and we reject those efforts, in the end the loss will be ours. The industrious worker who "gives 100%" deserves respect, for such an effort becomes our goal and model. Jesus challenged the people of his day, and ourselves as well, to raise our minds, hearts and efforts to the level which he demonstrated during the days he walked on this earth. Let us accept the challenge and improve our efforts on behalf of God's people. Our journey home has achieved a significant point; may we earnestly continue our walk to Good Friday, Easter and to eternal life.

Saturday Week IV

Readings: Jeremiah 11:18-20; John 7:40-53

Accepting Change in Our Lives

Oscar Romero was considered to be the perfect candidate for archbishop of San Salvador. Those in positions of power, both within the Church and in Salvadoran society, thought that with his academic background, Romero would hold fast to his established beliefs and former practices and not upset the status quo. When Romero assumed the position of archbishop he became in every respect the pastor of the local Church. He listened to all people, both those in power and those dominated by the oppressive government in the country. As he traveled through the land he observed many things that seemed inconsistent with the Gospel's message of love and peace. When he spoke to his fellow bishops and government officials about the need for change, his words fell on deaf ears; few, if any, were willing to open their eyes to the reality of the situation and accept the need to reform society.

Romero became an advocate for the poor and those who had no voice in El Salvador. The once mild-mannered cleric became a contemporary John the Baptist as he denounced the government's refusal to aid the poor and marginalized of society. Archbishop Romero changed his whole attitude and approach based on his experience, but others didn't accept this change. He was warned of impending danger, but he continued to speak out and voice his opposition to the evil he observed. Oscar Romero realized the need to change in order to serve the needs of all people—a belief which was not appreciated by the power structure which had selected him to lead the local Church. In March 1980 an assassin's bullet cut short his courageous stand.

Throughout the centuries, problems have plagued those who call for change. The prophets, whose writings we read in the Hebrew Scriptures, were never fully appreciated for the message they proclaimed. In today's first reading Jeremiah speaks of how he was unaware that others were plotting to kill him. Like an innocent lamb led to slaughter he trusted others, but now he calls upon God to act against his opponents. Jeremiah's message, like that of all the prophets, was not easy to accept because it called for change, reform and repentance. People generally do not like to be told that they are wrong; they resist change when the existing circumstances and environment protect them and their position.

In the Gospel we hear how people were sharply divided over Jesus' message. Like Jeremiah, the Lord called for change in Hebrew society. Jesus did not care if he was popular or gained acclaim by his message. Some people were impressed and even amazed at Jesus' message: "Never has anyone spoken like this" (Jn 7:46). Others, however, clinging to the law as their guide, ridiculed those who accepted Jesus' call for change and conversion. Their arrogance and ignorance about Jesus' origins blinded them to the reality that he is the Messiah.

Change is difficult for most people, whether it means a major shift of work place, home or attitude, or a more subtle move in habit or custom. We may find that change in others is even more of a challenge because it may force us, without our consent, to shift what we do, think or say. Change for the sake of change is not necessarily good, but change that shakes us up a bit, makes us think, and causes us to reflect upon our lives spurs us to growth. People like Oscar Romero, Jeremiah and Jesus challenged many with their message of change and reform. Let us listen to the cry of contemporary prophets and act upon their call to conversion. May the change that we experience in our lives transform us into better instruments of God's love and peace. Let us share the renewal of our lives so as to build more completely the kingdom of God in today's world.

Meditations for the Fifth Week of Lent

Sunday Week V (A)

Readings: Ezekiel 37:12-14; Romans 8:8-11; John 11:1-45

Jesus Unchains Us

He was chained, held bound in a life of torment and blasphemy. In the end, however, God would set him free. John Newton, a name probably unfamiliar to many of us, was born in July 1725 to a pious English woman and her seafaring husband. From his earliest days, young Newton was attracted to his father's side of the family and to the life at sea. Thus, when he was only eleven years old he became an apprentice aboard his father's vessel, a cargo ship which ferried products throughout the major ports of the Mediterranean region. At this time in his life John Newton did not know God. Those with whom he associated on his father's ship were mostly criminals, rogues and other "undesirables" of society, many of whom were sent to Captain Newton's ship as punishment for some offense in England.

When Newton was nineteen he became a midshipman on another vessel. After only one year, however, he was publicly flogged for insubordination. Despite this event, and probably with the help of his father, John managed to secure a commission. A few years later he commanded his own vessel, a slave trading ship, which ferried Africans from their native land to the American colonies. He excelled at what he did and carried out his duties with precision. Still, he felt chained and trapped; he was unable to release himself.

This all changed one night in 1748. That evening a vicious storm almost capsized Newton's slave ship. Waves crashed over the bow, tossing the ship about like a toy. Through the skill of the captain and his crew, the ship and all personnel were saved. The experience, however, changed Newton forever. He felt the chains that held him bound begin to weaken. It took seven more years, but finally in 1755 John Newton gave up the slave trade and his life at sea.

That same year he met John Wesley and George Whitefield, two Episcopal clergymen who at that time were the leaders in the Evangelical revival which would lead to the foundation of Methodism in the United States. In 1764 Newton himself was ordained an Episcopal priest. He became a well-known preacher and was the one of the first members of what later became known as the Abolitionist movement, with such leaders as Daniel O'Connell in Ireland and William Lloyd Garrison in the United States.

In 1779, Newton wrote some famous words, autobiographical in nature, that are familiar to us all. "Amazing grace, how sweet the sound that saved a wretch like me. I once was lost, but now I'm found, was blind but now I see." Yes, John Newton wrote the words to "Amazing Grace." He was held bound in a life he did not want. In the end, God set him free. The life of John Newton serves to illustrate what our readings describe today—God can set us free from all that binds us.

Today's Gospel is familiar to all of us. We might ask why Jesus, Martha, Mary and Lazarus were such good friends of Jesus. What was the nature of their relationship? We do not know the answers, but we do know that they were very close. Why then did Jesus linger for three days when he learned that one of his best friends was sick, possibly to the point of death? Would any of us delay a trip if we could go to the aid of one of our friends who needs us? Hopefully not. Jesus answers this question, however, saying that Lazarus' illness is to show God's glory. We might take that one step further and say that Jesus lingered so that the Spirit could set Lazarus and all people free from death, not just physical death, but more importantly spiritual death and ultimately eternal death. Jesus says, "I am the resurrection and the life" (Jn 11:25). Whoever believes in Jesus will never be without hope. Whoever believes in the Lord will never die without the Spirit.

Jesus wanted Martha, Mary and all those present, and you and I as well, to know that his presence is not so much to save us from physical death as it is to bring us to eternal life. Jesus restores hope and unchains us from all that holds us back from being the fullness of who we want to be. The words of Jesus at the end of the Gospel are powerful indeed, "Unbind him, and let him go" (Jn 11:44). Jesus removed the shackles, chains and the shroud of death from Lazarus. He can do that for all of us as well.

We know well that God has always been active on behalf of his people in releasing us from the bonds of this earth's existence. We remember that God broke the shackles of the Israelites in bondage in Egypt through the work of Moses. Later God sent the judges and the prophets, the Deborahs and the Esthers, the Isaiahs as well, to guide the people to a better life and understanding of

God's way. We hear from one of those major prophets in today's first reading. Ezekiel was writing to the Hebrews who were in bondage again. This time they were in exile in Babylon. Yes, the people were suffering from physical confinement and isolation from their homeland. But their psychological chains were probably greater. They were without hope and were living in despair. Many of the Hebrews thought that God had abandoned them. Ezekiel told the people that God will unshackle their chains and rescue them from their exile, their captivity, their grave, returning them to their land. God's faithfulness to his people will restore hope and break their bonds. A new day will dawn and a new spring will blossom.

Yes, God's rescue of the Hebrew people from the land of Babylon, and Jesus' raising Lazarus from the dead demonstrate the faithfulness of God in unleashing us from all that binds us. All of us are bound, dead in some way or another. Maybe some of us are held bound by the cares of this world, which have such a strong and popular attraction these days. For others a burden in our family, at work or in the community might have hold of us and will not let go. Others are chained by some situation which will not give release. Some may be prisoners of their past sins and think that nobody cares.

Our chains, our bonds, will give us a certain sense of dying. Lazarus was caught in the trap of physical death and perhaps other forms of death of which we are not aware. The Hebrews were victims of the death of despair, hopelessness and isolation. Through the action of Christ, who brings the light, as he reminds his apostles in today's Gospel, we are released from all that chains us. We only need to be open to the action of God in our lives. St. Paul says in today's second reading that the Spirit gives hope. The Spirit can release us from all that binds us. The walking dead, those who are held bound, are all around us. We need look no farther than ourselves. Jesus says, "Unbind them, and let them go." Jesus can untie us from all that chains us in this life. Let us give our lives over to the Lord. He can break the bonds that hold us in this life, so that in the end, we will be bound to God forever in the eternal life that we all hope to share!

Sunday Week V (B)

Readings: Jeremiah 31:31-34;
Hebrews 5:7-9; John 12:20-33

Dying to New Life

If you look up the word "paradox" in the dictionary you will find a definition that runs something like this: a statement which on first examination appears to be false, but on a closer reading is found to be true. Examples of paradoxes abound—I would like to share two, one from literature and one from the world of mathematics.

In the famous dialogue *Meno* by Plato, Socrates and his friend Meno are holding a deep discussion. Meno poses the following question, "Is it possible to know that which one has not learned?" Meno answers his own question by saying no. There is nothing that a person knows that has not been previously learned. Socrates, however, ponders this question, known as "Meno's Paradox," and says yes. Certain things are so innate to the human person that we know them without learning, such as the emotions of love.

The second paradox is from the world of mathematics. If you want to go from point A to point B, and you move exactly one-half of the remaining distance between the two points on each move, you will never arrive at your destination. At first glance you might say, that certainly cannot be correct; I must be able to figure this out. The statement is a paradox. If one can move only half the remaining distance each time, you will come close, infinitely close, but you will never arrive.

Although we can all probably think of many other paradoxes, we might ask, "What is the greatest paradox?" The answer most assuredly is Christianity. Christ himself is a paradox. Jesus is God, yet he is human at the same time. How is this possible? It is a mystery, yet it is the truth. It is a paradox. Most especially the teaching of Jesus, his message which forms the basis of our faith, is a paradox. In today's Gospel Jesus gives us the classic Christian paradox, "Unless a grain of wheat falls into the earth and dies, it remains just a single grain; but if it dies, it bears much fruit" (Jn 12:24). Again Jesus says the same thing in different words, "Those who love their life lose it, and those who hate their life in this world will keep it for eternal life" (Jn 12:25).

How is this possible? It seems like it can't be true, but it is. It is a paradox. Yes, Jesus' statement is true. More importantly, what does it mean for us? Do we need to die to find eternal life? Is our life here without merit? Are our daily efforts useless? Jesus' statement, this ultimate paradox, means that we must give our lives for others. This requires sacrifice. We are to give to others and we are to take less so that others may have some. It is done by sharing what we have in material things. In short, as the expression goes, it is to live simply so others may simply live.

How do we do this; how do we live for others? Jesus' example shows us that the principal way is through service. We are to serve those who are meek and lowly, those who seem to count for little in our world, such as the poor and homeless. Our ultimate goal should be to die in Christ and rise to a new, fuller and eternal life. But this does not mean that we are not accountable now. The Christian paradox operates not only at death, but it must be lived each day in our relationship with God and others.

In the Gospel Jesus clarifies the new covenant promise which Jeremiah speaks about. God has forged an unbreakable bond with his people. This bond is the Lord's commitment to the paradox. Jesus learned obedience through suffering, as the Letter to the Hebrews says (Heb 5:8), and this demonstrates his unity with us. He has given us a new way of life, a way which finds its direction by self-renunciation, sacrifice and service.

Jesus says in the Gospel that his hour has come. Our hour has come as well. It is our hour for action; it is our hour to renew our relationship with God. To die to self in this world produces many wonderful gifts which lead us to a fuller relationship with God and others.

Yes, Christianity is a paradox. Our life finds its fulfillment through death. Physical death will bring us to the presence of God and eternal life when God calls us to himself. But more importantly death to self produces much fruit now and makes the kingdom of God more manifest each day. Let us sacrifice ourselves and serve others. Let us die to self, as the Christian paradox calls us to do, and in the process find eternal life as well!

Sunday Week V (C)

Readings: Isaiah 43:16-21; Philippians 3:8-14; John 8:1-11

Growing through New Experiences

Dorothy Day was born on November 8, 1897, in Brooklyn, the eldest child of a roving newspaper sports writer and his wife. Due to her father's work the family moved often in her youth. In 1906 the Days were living in Berkeley, California when the great earthquake and subsequent fire destroyed a large portion of nearby San Francisco. Without work after this disaster, the Day family had to move again. They settled in Chicago where they rented a drab six-room tenement above a tavern on the South side. When Dorothy's father obtained a permanent position with the Chicago *Inter-Ocean* the family moved to a better home just north of the city.

Like all people Dorothy experienced life with its ecstasies and its problems. Each experience offered an opportunity, a challenge and at times a pitfall. Each experience asked her to make a choice. She could choose to learn and grow, or she could allow society to conquer her, retreating inside herself and shutting out the world. The choice was hers.

At seventeen Dorothy enrolled at the University of Illinois on a scholarship from the Hearst newspaper chain. The classes bored her, except English, which stimulated her interest in writing. She read voraciously, cutting classes and keeping odd hours in order to read more. She discovered socialism, which attracted her. Each experience was an opportunity to grow and helped develop her worldview which was socially conscious, outward looking, and open to possibilities.

After two years of college she returned to New York where she was hired as a reporter for socialist and communist newspapers. Life was difficult for Dorothy Day. She lived a Bohemian lifestyle, renting a small apartment in Manhattan's upper East Side. She shared her food with the rats that darted through the dingy room and with the homeless who slept outside her front door. She managed to eke out a living, all the while searching and running but never focused on a goal. A passing affair ended in an abortion; another romance led to marriage and to a divorce only one year later. A common-law marriage produced a daughter. She roamed to Hollywood, Mexico, New Orleans, then back to New York.

Floating, drifting, but always questioning and growing, she came to Washington, D.C. on December 8, 1932, to cover a hunger march for the Catholic weekly *America*. After her assignment was completed she came to the Shrine of the Immaculate Conception on that special Marian feast day to pray. As a recent convert to Catholicism she asked God for direction in her life. Dorothy wanted to discover the goal and the method to achieve it. It would not be long before God would answer her plea.

When she returned to New York her friends told her that a middle-aged man had been asking for her in her absence. This man, Peter Maurin, a French emigré to the United States via Canada, had been sent to Dorothy by George Shuster, managing editor of *Commonweal*, another Catholic weekly published in New York. Maurin had a new vision for the world, what he claimed would be its salvation. His plan had three parts. The first was to establish houses of hospitality to shelter and feed the homeless. The second part was to engage the mind through round table discussions on the important social issues of the day, led by some recognized expert in the field. Lastly, in support of the back-to-the-land movement, he advocated the foundation of farming communes for work and study. Thus in December 1932 an articulate woman searching for answers, Dorothy Day, and a man with a vision and plan, Peter Maurin, joined forces to establish the Catholic Worker Movement. They published their first newspaper on May 1, 1933. It sold for a penny. It stands as a primary example of the lay apostolate and Catholic Action prominent in the United States of the 1930s.

Dorothy Day's story is a very human tale. She experienced life with its highs and lows. She took risks, sometimes failing, but always learning and growing through the experience. She thought of others, not herself. In the end she found her goal and achieved it. Our readings today speak of how we need to let go of the past, to learn from and grow through the experiences of life. We are to race toward the prize which is Jesus Christ.

Being a prophet in ancient Israel was a difficult task. The prophets often had to deliver a hard message, which the people rejected. Prophets like Isaiah had to grow through the many difficulties of their lives. So too did the Hebrew people themselves have to grow through adversity. Writing to the people in exile in Babylon, the prophet tells them that they caused their own problems. Their inattention to Yahweh's will pushed them off the main road that leads to God. Through the words of the prophet, God reassures them that the past is forgotten, now all is new. God will be with them so they can make a fresh beginning, like the river makes a new beginning of life in the desert. The great challenge for the people is to learn from and grow through their experiences. God will be with them, but they must choose new life and growth; God will not force them.

In the Gospel the woman caught in adultery is like the Hebrew community in exile. The woman's own actions have placed her in this difficult situation. She is in danger of death, since her sin is punishable by stoning, but Jesus says that the past is forgotten, for the woman and her accusers. One must move on and accomplish great things. As Jesus says, "Go your way, and from now on do not sin again" (Jn 8:11).

The trials and tribulations of life have battered all of us. Sometimes our own actions and words have sidetracked us and other times things totally beyond our control push us off the desired path. But no matter how smooth or unhassled the road may be for some, or riddled with obstacles for others, all of us have three options when new experiences come our way. We can pass by the new experience. After all, most of us already have too much on our slate; we don't need an added item. On the other hand, we may slow down when a new experience occurs. We might look for a while and even listen for a bit, but then we move on, somewhat better for the time spent. Finally, we may stop on the road. We look carefully and listen well. It may require a change in direction, but offers an opportunity to grow, to learn and begin anew.

New experiences come to challenge all of us. Like the Hebrews and the woman caught in adultery who were asked to forget the past, to grow and move on, so too are we challenged to reach for new heights. All of us bear the scars of this life, its bumps and bruises. We all have done things we would like to forget. Jesus tells us to drop the baggage, grow through the experience, and follow him. For us who live a rather comfortable existence, where we can look forward with anticipation and joy to tomorrow, next week and even next year, the experience will differ from that of our brothers and sisters who occupy our inner city slums. Our experiences will differ, but God asks us to look at each new experience as an opportunity for growth, a graced moment to learn. We are to forget the past, the errors of yesterday, and armed with new possibilities go forward to meet our future challenges.

Paul's image of the race in today's second reading shows us the goal. We are to look to the future, to focus on the ultimate prize—union with God. But along the road many new experiences will challenge us. Dorothy Day used the opportunities sent her way to discover the right road and her method to meet her goal. The Hebrews and the adulterous woman also were able to grow through pain and difficulty in order to find greater peace. How can we find the road that leads to God? One way to start is through the process of reconciliation. Reconciliation is one of the sacraments, the seven great signs of God's love. But it is more fundamentally a journey which begins by looking inside ourselves and accepting both the goodness and the sinfulness we find. Then we can begin to experience reconciliation with our sisters and brothers and ultimately reconciliation with God.

As our Lenten journey draws to its climax, let us be open to the experiences which come to us in our daily journey. Let us learn to meet the challenges and to grow. May the past be forgotten as we race to our final goal—life with Jesus, our brother, Savior and Lord.

Monday Week V

Readings: Daniel 13:1-9, 15-17, 19-30, 33-62; John 8:1-11

God Can Work Things Out

Sometimes life might knock us down, but we can always get up again, even if it means hobbling with a crutch. In baseball if the home team is behind by five runs and they have two outs at the bottom of the ninth inning, most of the fans will stream out of the grandstands, assuming that the game is lost. Yet in the 1986 world series a similar situation faced the New York Mets. The Boston Red Sox were ready to close out the series in the sixth game and appeared to have things locked up, but the Mets charged from behind in the ninth inning, won game six, and went on to capture the world championship. In 1948 every political poll in the country predicted President Harry Truman's demise; the Republican candidate, Thomas Dewey, would certainly beat him. Yet, when the votes were tallied Truman astounded everyone and carried the election. The criminal justice system in the United States tries to safeguard the rights of the innocent. However, no system is foolproof and sometimes an innocent person is convicted. Today, however, new criminal science techniques, such as DNA testing, have been used to prove the innocence of several people convicted of heinous crimes.

No situation is hopeless. If we hold out until the end, the sun will eventually stream in. Our Scripture readings today show us two situations, which, although somewhat similar, have important differences in their common discovery of hope from the depths of despair. Susanna was trapped in a "no win" situation. If she gave in to the lust of the two elders she would commit a grave sin, but if she held out she would be condemned by the law since her accusers were well respected in the Hebrew community. By refusing to commit sin Susanna made the right choice, and thus God stirred the heart of Daniel to rescue her. The situation looked bleak, but God rewarded Susanna's integrity.

The Gospel story differs in some important aspects. While the woman, like Susanna, is accused of sexual misconduct, the text doesn't indicate that she was innocent. On the contrary, the scribes and Pharisees lead forth a woman "who had been caught in adultery" (Jn 8:3). Hebrew law stipulated stoning for her transgression, but Jesus' presence gives her hope. Unlike Susanna who was innocent, this woman seems to be guilty, but Jesus demonstrates that mercy outweighs strict adherence to the law. Some Scripture scholars today say that when Jesus twice bent down to trace on the ground he was writing the sins of the woman's accusers in the dirt. By the law it is probable that all present deserved punishment of some sort, but Jesus exonerates the woman to demonstrate mercy to her and the possibility of forgiveness to all who possess a contrite heart. The Lord grants pardon, but he cautions the woman to avoid this sin in the future.

Situations which appear hopeless or fill us with despondency are part of life; we can't escape from this reality. Much more important than baseball or political elections are situations where human life is placed in jeopardy. Today's readings show us how to place our hope in God at all times. God is always present, observes our situation, and guides our direction in life. Susanna prayed for the Lord's help and Daniel was sent to right the injustice. The woman in the Gospel knew her guilt but accepted Jesus' mercy and admonition to do better in the future. Let us demonstrate our faith in God's guiding hand, place our confidence in the Lord's presence, and accept God's loving mercy when situations leave us empty and hopeless. Let us walk alongside Jesus as our Lenten journey to God continues.

Tuesday Week V

Readings: Numbers 21:4-9; John 8:21-30

A Challenging "Mission Impossible"

Several years ago the television program *Mission Impossible* attracted many viewers. Each episode began the same way. The chief of the Impossible Missions Force, or IMF, was observed in some sequestered and remote spot where he would discover a large manila envelope filled with printed information and photographs. He also found a tape recording which described the next mission that had been assigned to the IMF. The information, photos and tape described the mission in full detail. At the end of the tape a voice would always say, "Should you choose to accept this mission and be caught the secretary will disavow any knowledge of your actions." The tape would then self-destruct and the program would begin.

Moses must have thought that his task of leading the Hebrews from bondage in Egypt to the Promised Land was mission impossible, but unlike the IMF he had no choice but to accept God's challenge. From the beginning the assignment tested Moses' will, strength, perseverance and faith. God was with him the entire way and performed many signs and miracles, both in Egypt and the Sinai desert. But Moses was forced to deal with the Hebrew people who were anything but cooperative and often refused to believe. Time after time they complained to Moses about every aspect of their life. As we hear in today's reading they griped they were tired of eating the manna sent by God. The Lord wearied of the people's constant complaints and punished them with serpents which "bit the people, so that many Israelites died" (Num 21:6). Despite all the trouble which the people had already caused for Moses, he still interceded with God for them, who healed them through the bronze serpent.

Jesus also must have felt his mission was impossible, but he never wavered from the task the Father had given him. Jesus came to teach a new way of life. Today's Gospel describes how he taught about his close relationship with the Father, and thus taught the people about their need to link themselves intimately with God. Jesus was probably frustrated that his hearers seldom understood what he was trying to say. Jesus told them that when he would be lifted up (on the cross) they will come to know who he is. Thus, Jesus predicted his death, but few if any understood his words.

The world today is a complicated place and we may often think that we are on "mission impossible." Demands seem only to increase; they never subside. Family, community, work and Church all ask something of us. We want and seem to need thirty hours each day to complete our tasks. It is easy to become frustrated and even to surrender to forces that dominate our life. But there is a way to accomplish what seems to be mission impossible—to link our actions with those of Jesus, as he associated himself with the Father. We might not be able to accomplish every single task today or even tomorrow. The demands will only become greater and thus we might fall further behind. But if we act in communion with the Lord, then our tasks become God's work which is not bounded by human time and space. God asks only our honest effort, to do the best with the gifts, time, resources and opportunities we have. Without God pressures will mount, frustration levels rise, and we will never feel up to the task. But with God the impossible becomes possible. Let us tackle the "mission impossible" of life, but let us do so in alliance with Jesus. The difficult we can do today but with God the impossible can be accomplished tomorrow.

Wednesday Week V

Readings: Daniel 3:14-20, 91-92, 95;
John 8:31-42

The Truth That Sets Us Free

Freedom is a precious gift that the human spirit requires to flourish. All people long to be free and to enjoy the wondrous and bountiful gifts of God without being chained to burdens which stifle the spirit. Freedom is the opposite of slavery. On one level, to be free means that the shackles of life have been removed and we are able to go where we want, do what we choose, and say what we feel. But freedom of choice is given us not so that we might do what we want, but so that we might choose the good. Most people believe that freedom of choice breaks the grip of slavery, which can then no longer hold us captive. In a physical sense this may be true, but humans are slaves to many things and most of us are totally unaware of it.

In some countries freedom of expression and action are considered basic rights. As free as we might seem, however, most of us are slaves to situations, peoples, attitudes and even events. Many people are chained by situations in the home. The abuse of spouses and children is often not reported because people are enslaved to another; they cannot make a break for fear of what might happen or uncertainty about striking out on one's own. Some people are slaves to attitudes which may have been developed many years ago. We think one way about people, politics, society and the Church, and we feel content to keep our blinders on to block out any possibility for change. In this way we chain ourselves and limit our possibilities. Some people are slaves to events of the past—hurt feelings, painful or broken relationships, sickness and death. If we are not careful, such things can drag us down and smother us. We become slaves in many ways while we live in freedom.

With keen insight, Jesus realized that people often fall into slavery while thinking they are free. Jesus says in the Gospel that we must know the truth and the truth will set us free. Living according to the teachings of the Lord makes us his disciples and helps us discover the truth. In another passage Jesus tells Thomas, "I am the way, and the truth, and the life" (Jn 14:6). If we know Jesus then we possess the truth, and this truth, this knowledge of God's Son, will set us free. Jesus realized that his hearers, proud and free people, were nonetheless enslaved to many things. Their response to the letter of the law chained them to the past, excluding the present and the future. They were also slaves to sin because they refused to believe that Jesus came to free them from their transgressions.

The well-known story of Shadrach, Meshach and Abednego illustrates how knowledge of God makes us free. These three men possessed full confidence in the Lord and refused to fall down and worship the golden statue as King Nebuchadnezzar demanded. They risked being bound and thrown into the white-hot furnace as a punishment. In reward for their faith God sent an angel to rescue them from the furnace and guide them to safety. The truth set them free.

Jesus is the source of all truth. He breaks the chains that enslave us. The power of evil and sin surround us, but as the fire that threatened to consume the three young men could not stand up against their belief, so too can our knowledge of God, the truth, defeat the evil which chains us. Freedom is a precious gift that must never be taken for granted, especially when we think we live in an environment of liberty and justice for all. Our Lenten journey is rapidly reaching its climax and we must not be found in chains when the end comes. Let us reflect on the ways that we, by choice or outside pressure, are enslaved to other things. Let us seek Jesus, the truth, and the truth will set us free!

Thursday Week V

Readings: Genesis 17:3-9; John 8:51-59

Completing God's Plan of Salvation

Giacomo Puccini was one of the greatest opera composers who ever lived. His melodic and glorious music, written for and performed in the great opera houses of the world, has delighted people for more than a century. Puccini was given many great gifts by God, but certainly his musical ability was the greatest. He gained fame, not only in his native land of Italy, but throughout the world. It was quite common to hear people along the streets of any of the world's large cities whistling or humming one of the many popular melodies from such great works as *Tosca, La Boheme, Madame Butterfly, Manon Lescaut* and *Gianni Schicchi.*

Toward the end of his life Puccini took on a challenge: the composition of another great opera to complete his master plan. Using a libretto written by fellow Italian Renato Simoni, who adapted a work of the 18th-century Venetian playwright Carlo Gozzi, Puccini tackled the composition of *Turandot.* It is the story of a gallant young man, Calaf, in his efforts to win the hand in marriage of a stern, mysterious and seemingly cold Chinese Princess named Turandot. Puccini was in his sixties when he began to compose the opera. For four years he labored long and hard, but ill-health plagued him. He was running out of time; God would soon call him to return home.

Puccini did return home to God, but left the final

work of his master plan uncompleted. Because he was a famous composer, Puccini had many friends, including a cadre of loyal students who were known as his disciples. These young men and women would not allow their master's great work, his *magnum opus,* to lie unfinished. They gathered together, studied the text of the opera, and, when ready, began the difficult task of finishing their master's work. In 1926, two years after his death, Puccini's greatest work, *Turandot,* was performed for the first time. It was done at Milan's La Scala Opera House with the most famous conductor of the day, Arturo Toscanni, at the podium. When the opera reached the point where Puccini's work ended Toscanni paused, set down his baton, and said, "Thus far the master wrote, but he died." After a moment of silence Toscanni again picked up his baton, turned to the audience, and with tears in his eyes said, "But his disciples finished his work." To thunderous applause the opera continued; Puccini's master plan had been completed.

God's master plan of salvation had a long genesis that was not completed even in Jesus' time on earth. The covenant made with Abraham was one of the first great pacts of God's plan. God chose Abraham's descendants to be a people uniquely his own. It is from this community that God's plan of salvation would be born and mature. God would build a great nation situated in fertile country and ruled by kings. The people would have the land of Canaan as their permanent possession. God asked for adherence to this covenant and promised to be present, protect the people, and provide for their needs. The people, in turn, must worship God alone.

God's master plan found its fulfillment and climax in

Jesus. Christ came to teach us about God. As we have heard before in our readings and again in today's Gospel, Jesus speaks of his close association with the Father. Jesus knows the Father but his hearers reject this claim. They see Jesus only as a man; they cannot go deeper to perceive his divinity and the importance of his message. Thus, although Jesus' incarnation and life brought God's master plan to its greatest height, the work still was not completed.

We who bear the name Christian have the duty, as did the disciples of Puccini, to complete our Master's work. There is much to be done in building God's kingdom on earth, but we have been provided with the things we need for the task. God has given all of us many talents and gifts which are to be used to further God's reign in our world. Some are gifted as writers or speakers who can promulgate the word to others. Others have been given gifts of great intelligence to discover new things and help explain many of the mysteries of our world. Still others labor in God's vineyard with physical tasks. All of us, through our common vocation to holiness, have been assigned to do our share to complete God's master plan. We do so by directing our efforts along lines that will draw ourselves and others closer to God.

The great Christian paradox, that life comes from death, is rapidly approaching as our Lenten journey continues. God's master plan required that Jesus come to our world, suffer, die and rise so that death would no longer have any permanent hold on the human race. In a similar way God asks us to die to self and to build the kingdom and thereby complete the Master's work. As sons and daughters of the Lord, let us contemplate our role in God's plan and do our share to complete it.

Friday Week V

Readings: Jeremiah 20:10-13; John 10:31-42

Preparing for the Challenge of Life

Each day life challenges us, testing who we are as human beings. In school, the challenge comes mainly in the form of examinations. No one enjoys tests, which cause worry, anxiety and sometimes lost sleep. Exams are necessary, however, not only for the teacher to evaluate progress but for the student to organize thoughts and articulate new knowledge. Student examinations force one to dig deeper, push harder and ask questions so as to derive the maximum benefit from education.

When we're out of school, challenges come in new ways. Constant evaluation takes place at work. Employees face scrutiny from peers and supervisors alike. First impressions are formed on the basis of punctuality, demeanor, appropriate dress and personality. Whether we pass muster often depends on how we initially strike people and thus we must rise to that challenge. Greater demands await us in our work tasks. Supervisors evaluate workers on the basis of such qualities as precision, dependability and dedication.

To meet the challenges of life one must prepare. An examination in school requires study. Few if any can pass tests without reading assignments, reviewing notes and working a few practice problems. At work we need to prepare for evaluations. More importantly we must ask advice, seek counsel, and do what is necessary to meet the challenges. Preparation is absolutely necessary to pass the tests and derive the maximum benefit from what we do.

God daily challenges and puts us to the test, not to trip us up, but rather to prod us to move, grow and maximize our potential. Without challenge we can stagnate; we need to be pushed, nudged and tested. God challenged the prophets of old, like Jeremiah in today's reading, with a difficult mission which many people rejected. The prophet speaks of how all around him are watching for any misstep on his part. They challenge his words and constantly put him to the test. With God's help, Jeremiah has prepared for his task, and thus he is ready for anything. His enemies will not be able to trap him for God will uphold the prophet. Jeremiah is confident that the Lord's presence in his life will spell failure for those who reject God and challenge his message. Preparation has led to triumph.

In his life and ministry, Jesus constantly faced challenges. The Jewish authorities rejected the Lord's claim to be the Son of God and threatened to stone him. Jesus performed good deeds, preached a message of peace, love and reconciliation, and formed a community, a Church, to continue his work after his death. Jesus was always prepared for the trials forced upon him. As the time of Jesus' passion drew near the tests came more frequently and grew more severe, but his union with God the Father allowed him to triumph.

Our Lenten journey is a time to be challenged. From the beginning God has asked us to look at every aspect of our life and to see where we need to move, what we need to do, and how we might accomplish these changes.

Preparation is the key to all life's challenges, especially those which come from God. Prayer is integral to our preparation; it is the first step in meeting God's challenge. We must speak with and listen to God to find solutions to the tests that come our way. Our preparation also requires reflection on our daily life and being open to opportunities and possibilities. When we are settled in and at ease with our relationship with God then we have taken the necessary steps to prepare ourselves for the challenges and tests of human life. As the days of this sacred season begin to draw to their climax let us earnestly continue our preparation to meet the Lord on our journey home.

Saturday Week V

Readings: Ezekiel 37:21-28; John 11:45-57

Unity with God and One Another

The scientific principle of entropy states that things in nature will randomly yet naturally tend toward disorder. Physics may explain the reality of the observable world, but it cannot tell us why greater harmony is found in unity. Examples abound of how items find greater usefulness, strength and peace by working together as one. Alloy metals, such as bronze and brass, which were probably discovered by accident thousands of years ago, are stronger, longer-lasting, and more durable than either of their components. River systems, such as the Mississippi, are more useful when several tributaries and smaller rivers come together as one. People as well find greater harmony, strength and opportunity by acting as a single unit. In the United States, fifty independent and sovereign governments believe that it is in their best interest to be under the overall control of one legislative body, the Congress, and one executive officer, the President. Nations themselves seek unity through international organizations such as the United Nations, NATO and the Common Market.

In the plan of salvation history God used the fact that greater strength, sense of purpose, and harmony can be created by seeking unity. The Hebrews had moved in and out of their relationship with God. Their lack of faithfulness landed them in exile in Babylon where they had much time to contemplate the errors of their ways. Jeremiah writes to the exiles in today's reading. Their lack of faith was often manifest in a selfish attitude which created divisions in the community when the rich and powerful placed a barrier between themselves and the common people. The prophets often challenged the leaders of both Israel and Judah concerning the oppression of the poor, but their warnings generally went unheeded. Those in power were content to have their way; exploitation of others did not disturb them. Despite their lack of faith, Jeremiah predicts that God will return the people to their home. God will heal the break caused by division of the people into two nations; they will become one in name and attitude.

Jesus also knew the great value of bringing unity to the Jewish community. Thus he was willing to die, as Caiaphas states, as a sacrificial lamb, for the benefit of the nation. Jesus came to bring people to wholeness and he told them that the only way this was possible was for people to care for one another. The Lord gathered a special group of twelve and later he sent out a further seventy-two to continue the mission. Jesus realized that the task was too big and complex for any person to act alone. The Trinity—the Father, Son, and Holy Spirit—acts as a community of love to create, redeem and sanctify our world. It is now our task to seek closer unity so as to generate greater strength, purpose and harmony in building God's kingdom in our world.

Human society must be continually built up in a model of community in order to fulfill Jesus' command to make disciples of all nations. We can join together at work, in our communities and in our families to strengthen each others' efforts and make them more fruitful. Alloy metals, rivers and national structures show us how greater unity can bring many benefits. Let us imitate this idea, manifest most profoundly in the unity of our God. Jesus' prayer must be our goal: "...that they may all be one. As you, Father, are in me and I am in you, may they also be in us, so that the world may believe that you have sent me" (Jn 17:21).

Meditations for Holy Week

Palm Sunday

Readings: Matthew 21:1-11; Isaiah 50:4-7; Philippians 2:6-11; Matthew 26:14–27:66 (A); Mark 14:1–15:47 (B); Luke 22:14–23:56 (C)

The Paradox of Death

The motion picture *Patton,* produced in 1970, won eight academy awards, including one for George C. Scott as best actor, who portrayed the famous American World War II general. The film opens in a rather odd manner. Patton, in full military regalia, stands atop a platform, addressing his troops before they enter battle. In the course of his comments he states, "Some people say it is glorious to die for your country. But I say that the objective of war is to make the other guy die for his country." That statement says something very indicative about what we as a society think of death. We see it as something to be shunned and avoided; it is dishonorable to die. Certainly anyone in a normal situation wants to live and desires that all friends and loved ones remain healthy and active. Still, for the Christian, one's attitude toward death must be different. We have been given life by God for the ultimate purpose of returning to our Creator. We are on a journey which leads to God, but can only arrive at the final destination through death.

Lent is also a journey which in many ways simulates our whole life path, from birth to death. We began this season on Ash Wednesday when we received the ashes which not only speak of our mortality but also of the journey that we started.

During this season we have gone to the desert with Jesus to be tested by Satan with the great temptations which have haunted humans for ages—power, wealth and prestige. We next went to a high mountain, with Jesus, Peter, James and John and we saw the Lord transfigured. It was a momentary external transformation, but what did that miraculous event in Jesus' life do to transform us on the inside? We have walked alongside Jesus in the day's heat and the evening's coolness, experiencing along the way his triumphs and his difficulties. Now we enter the final part of the journey, a road that leads to death, but also to resurrection and eternal life.

During Holy Week we relive a series of events about which our readings speak today. Jesus is welcomed with hosannas and palms as the great king when he enters the city of Jerusalem. Yet, we already know the end of the story. In five days he will be crucified, but he will rise again! The mystery of the Easter Triduum, the principle which is so basic to Christianity, yet was totally absent from Patton's speech, is that something wonderful can be created from the tragedy of death. Jesus is the suffering servant of the prophet Isaiah, who foretold that Jesus would be abused and mocked, rejected and spurned. Jesus is also the God-man spoken of in the famous Christological hymn of St. Paul in his Letter to the Philippians. Although God, Jesus emptied himself of his divinity to take human form and experience death on a cross. Yes, this suffering servant, this God-man, enters Jerusalem in triumph. He eats dinner with his disciples and then willingly chooses death for the freedom and salvation of sinful humanity. He was an innocent victim of hatred. Yet this same Jesus will rise and bring all people for all time the possibility of salvation.

Jesus' journey to death and resurrection must give us hope. It is a hope born in difficulty, which says, despite the paradox, that life can only come from death. If we are willing to continue the Lenten journey with Jesus to the end, if we will walk with him, then we too will find good through evil, triumph through defeat, and life through death. Let us continue our walk with Jesus; let us stay close to him and in the process find life without end!

Monday of Holy Week

Readings: Isaiah 42:1-7; John 12:1-11

Fulfilling Our Purpose

The birth of a child brings great joy to all, but especially to the parents who have anticipated the great and blessed event for nine months. When children are born it is natural for parents to dream about the future of their child. They are filled with hopes, dreams and thoughts about what the child will do and where he or she will live. Some have the future mapped out for their children, whose purpose in life has been determined before they have taken one step or uttered a single coherent word. All of us have a purpose in life that is seldom known at the outset but is gradually revealed over time. Sometimes what we do in life coincides with the ideas and hopes of our parents, but usually this is not the case.

Ultimately the purpose of each person is to return to God, from whom we came. Along the road we will experience different paths, challenges and opportunities that will take us to far off locations, place us in situations we never desired, and force us to do things for which we have little training or apparent desire. All that we do and the various means we use to accomplish our daily tasks are directed toward the purpose of returning home. Many paths lead to that one goal.

We have entered upon Holy Week, the most sacred time of the Church year. For the past five weeks we have been on a special journey preparing for the events which will culminate this week. This special sub-journey of life has provided many possibilities but none is greater than the opportunity to review our life, honestly evaluate where we are on the path, and move forward to prepare to celebrate the Paschal Mystery. Jesus has walked this road with us and now he comes to the climax of the trip. Like all of us whose purpose is to return to God, Jesus makes a final preparation for his journey home. He spent his time on earth teaching, preaching, witnessing and working to build God's kingdom. The end of the road approaches; Jesus' ultimate purpose of returning to the Father draws near. In today's reading we hear the first of five "suffering servant" passages in which Isaiah prophesied about Jesus' final hours. Christ would suffer but he would do so willingly. "He will not cry or lift up his voice, or make it heard in the street" (Is 42:2). An ignoble death faced Jesus at the end of his journey, but he would be prepared in advance for it, as we hear in the Gospel. Mary anointed the Lord for burial before the fact; her action flowed from her love for God who first loved her.

We do not know what the future holds for us, but we do know that the end of the journey, both now in Lent and at the end of our days, is union with God. The immediate journey has an end point that is known and for which we can prepare, but our final call home is known to God alone. Along the road home we will meet detours, obstacles and roadblocks, which we must overcome to reach our goal. What we find along our path, whether it is the path picked out at our birth, the direct opposite or something in between, will eventually lead us back to God, if we direct ourselves toward this goal. As

Holy Week continues let us contemplate ways that we can better prepare for the events which now are so close. Our methods will be different but equally important. Let us voluntarily walk the road with Jesus, our brother, friend and Lord.

Tuesday of Holy Week

Readings: Isaiah 49:1-6; John 13:21-33, 36-38

The Measure of Success

All people seek success in life. We want all our endeavors, whether in our personal life, professional work, interaction with community or ministry in the Church, to succeed at a level which allows us to feel good about what we've accomplished. Success can be measured in a number of ways, some of which are quantitative and others which are intangible. We know we have been successful at work by getting good evaluations, promotions and higher pay. Success in relationships is more difficult to measure but can be observed by how people demonstrate love for one another, willingly sacrifice themselves for each other, or seek the enrichment of someone's company.

In life we measure success against failure with the constant hope that when the final tally is made, we'll have more marks in the success column. It is impossible to traverse the hurdles of life without failing sometimes. Sometimes failure stems more from the situation, other people's mistakes or the evil present in the world than with our own personal error, fault or defeat. But whatever the reason, failure causes great pain. We want to succeed in the various tasks of life and we exert much effort to reach this goal, but difficulties can arise that defeat us, no matter how great our effort.

The prophets who preceded the Lord Jesus himself knew well from their own experiences that defeat is part of life. Isaiah writes to the Hebrews in exile and reflects upon his task of proclaiming God's message and that most of the community did not heed his words. Isaiah was called from his mother's womb, but initially his work did not bear fruit; the prophet felt the pain of defeat. Although he thought he had toiled in vain and uselessly spent his strength, he came to realize that he would reach his ultimate success, his reward with the Lord. Moreover, in time Israel would be restored to its homeland and become a light to all nations. Isaiah's defeat would be turned to triumph with God's help.

Jesus came to our earth with a master plan for success. In his ministry he reached out to all people with a message of love, peace and justice. Along the way he chose followers who would continue his work after his return to God. During Holy Week we remember the last days of Jesus' life on earth, the final episodes in his ministry. Like all of us Jesus wanted to be successful and certainly he fulfilled his mission. But as the Gospel tells us today Jesus also suffered defeat and it came at the hands of his most trusted and loyal friends, his apostles. Jesus knew from the beginning that one of them would betray his cause, but it must still have caused him pain. Possibly even more hurtful was Peter's denial, which Jesus also knew would occur. The leader of the fledgling Church caused much pain for its founder. Peter must have been both a huge success and a dismal disappointment for Jesus. Through it all Jesus knew that he would triumph, but his victory came through death.

Success and failure, as part of daily life, come to us in various ways and at different times. We must diligently work to succeed, but even then defeat can come our way.

We need to keep our sights set on the ultimate success, the last victory which we seek and for which we prepare in this sacred season—union with God. The rapidly approaching days of Jesus' supreme sacrifice and triumph remind us that although defeat and failure may come our way we can move beyond them and triumph, if we are willing to take the risk, walk the road, and endure the pain. Let us look for ways to claim triumph from defeat as we await Jesus' ultimate success and the end of our own journey home to God.

Wednesday of Holy Week

Readings: Isaiah 50:4-9; Matthew 26:14-25

Betrayal or Loyalty: Which Do You Choose?

Betrayal is a human action which all find distasteful. We generally think of this term with respect to acts of treason against one's nation, desertion in the line of duty, or apostasy from the Faith. In the history of the United States we remember the infamous actions of Benedict Arnold during the Revolutionary War, who betrayed the colonies in support of the British. Arnold's name has become synonymous with betrayal. The case of Ethel and Julius Rosenberg, the only American civilians ever executed for treason, is another famous example of betrayal.

Loyalty is the opposite of betrayal. Society esteems the virtue of loyalty, which crowns all relationships. Loyalty to nation and flag, family, friends, community and Church commands people's respect and is the goal which all must seek in their lives. Although noble, loyalty is up to us; no one can force our hand to comply with rules, orders or demands. Sometimes people are loyal because it is expected but most remain faithful because a person, nation or ideal commands respect. People are seldom loyal to those who have hurt them, demonstrated disrespect, or refused to be faithful.

Today's readings speak of betrayal and loyalty, contrasting the human and divine response to situations. Judas received an offer to betray the Lord and when the opportunity presented itself he made his decision. Why

Judas chose to turn away from Jesus is not obvious; the only motivation appears to be money, the thirty pieces of silver. Maybe Judas foresaw the failure of Jesus' mission and wanted to get something out of all the time he had spent traveling with the Lord. Perhaps Judas no longer believed. Human greed may have gotten the best of him; it happens to many of us. Jesus had done no wrong nor injured anyone, yet he was betrayed by one of his chosen twelve, those in theory most likely to remain faithful.

In contrast to the human reaction of Judas, Jesus, God incarnate, remains loyal to the end. In prophetic prose Isaiah speaks of how the suffering servant will not rebel, not turn back. This man of God will willingly give himself over to buffets, spitting and other insults. The servant will be loyal to all, no matter the cost, even those who will turn away from him. But the servant is confident that in the end he will not be disgraced because God is with him, upholding the right against the evil which appears to surround him.

Loyalty is difficult especially in a world where betrayal is so pervasive and even acceptable. We seldom hear about major betrayals of nation or Church, but if we are not cautious we can betray people and ideals quite easily. When a friend, colleague or family member asks us for assistance, loyalty suggests that we will be faithful and meet our commitments. We betray our relationships with others, however, when we idly talk about people in uncharitable ways, refuse to reach out when there is a need, or purposely injure another's reputation. The betrayal of ideals happens readily if we forget our Christian constitution which mandates honesty, charity and faithfulness in our daily activities. We can easily betray God by failing to make God the top priority in our life, placing the things and peoples of the world above the one who created all.

Our Lenten journey of preparation for our return to God has ended. Tomorrow the Church enters the sacred Triduum to celebrate the paschal mystery—the passion, death and resurrection of the Lord. Let us center ourselves today in God's love and be mindful of our need to be loyal servants in response to Jesus' faithfulness to us. God has extended an invitation and now awaits our response.

Holy Thursday

Readings: Exodus 12:1-8, 11-14;
1 Corinthians 11:23-26; John 13:1-15

A People of Tradition

We are a people of tradition who celebrate customs in our families, society and religion. Families celebrate special days in unique ways. Each family has its tradition for gathering to celebrate holidays such as Christmas and Thanksgiving; birthdays, anniversaries and other significant events also bring families together to share and celebrate life and tradition. Society has its traditions as well. We have our system of laws and courts, a tradition handed down from the framers of the Declaration of Independence and the Constitution. Society celebrates national holidays in a customary manner. Traditions are handed on from one generation to another. We keep them alive through our attitudes and actions.

This night throughout the Christian world we enter into the most significant tradition of our faith, the celebration of the Easter Triduum. We celebrate the Paschal Mystery—the passion, death and resurrection of our Lord Jesus Christ. Our readings describe how this tradition has its roots in the Passover ritual of our spiritual ancestors, the Jewish people.

The Book of Exodus describes Passover. Jews today remember their tradition, their heritage, in the celebration of the seder meal. This solemn remembrance commemorates God's action in salvation history as he delivered the people from their bondage in Egypt. God, the ever-faithful one, was always there to rescue the Hebrews and to release them from their bonds. This significant tradition is still celebrated with much solemnity.

Christianity certainly has a vast tradition as well. All four Gospels mention the account of the Last Supper, but only the synoptics describe the institution of the Eucharist on this day. St. Paul, by telling others what he himself learned, is our other source of what happened that evening; he passed on the tradition of the Eucharist, which continues each day throughout the world. Christians gather to remember what Jesus did and taught. We also remember his death, which has become salvific for all of us.

We hear about another tradition in today's Gospel. St. John wants us to know that there is more to the Christian tradition concerning the Last Supper than the Eucharist. We learn in this Gospel of the tradition of service. Jesus initiates a new tradition with his actions at the Last Supper. The Lord washes the feet of his apostles, his closest followers, and he tells them and all of us to do the same.

In a society which is filled with injustice, poverty and crime, how can we answer Jesus' call to a life of service? We can wash the feet of others who enter our lives, especially those who exist on the fringes or suffer the most. We wash the feet of others in many ways. The most important way is through service and works of mercy. We need to become the servants of others. The service we render to others should become our tradition. This day let us remember the special traditions we have, and endeavor to live the new tradition of service in all that we do and say.

Good Friday

Readings: Isaiah 52:13—53:12; Hebrews 4:14-16; 5:7-9; John 18:1—19:42

Why Do People Suffer?

Why do people suffer? Why do pain, problems and suffering abound in the world? We believe that God is all good, all love, full of compassion and all powerful. This is how we define God. Since this is true, why do people suffer? Why do wars exist and why are innocent people killed? Why do public officials sink into corruption, causing others not only to lose faith in the individual, but in the system as well? Why do people fight one another because of the color of their skin, their political preference or religious belief?

For me the basic answer to these challenging questions is personal choice, our free will to say "yes" or "no" to God at any time in any way. Søren Kierkegaard, the famous 19th-century existentialist philosopher and theologian, once wrote, "Faith is a matter of choice, our personal decision in finding God." This personal decision, our free will, is why the world suffers. Free will allows the drunk to drive and kill others. Free will allows people in public service to break the law and thus corrupt the system. Free will isolates certain members and groups on the fringe of society, barring them from full participation. Free will moves us closer to or further from God. As Kierkegaard wrote, faith is our choice.

On Good Friday we remember suffering and pain, but this day has much more to offer. Our readings speak of Jesus' suffering, pain and death. More importantly, however, we need to ask, "Why did Jesus have to die?" Jesus did not have to die; he chose to die, so that we could find life. Jesus' salvific death, efficacious for all people of all time, came about of his own free will.

Isaiah again speaks of the suffering servant who freely chose to die. The servant's appearance attracted no one; he was a man of suffering and pain. As the servant gives his life, the will of God is accomplished through him. The sacrifice of the servant will win pardon for the offenses of others. The Letter to the Hebrews says that through his free will Jesus suffered in order to learn obedience (cf. Heb 5:8). Jesus chose to become human so that he could bring us salvation.

John's passion narrative describes the ultimate act of love and free choice that Jesus made for us. Jesus died for others, for you and me. Unlike the synoptic versions of the Gospel, St. John sees Jesus' exaltation in his death; the cross becomes his throne. For John, Jesus becomes king on the tree, not in his resurrection. For most all of us this sounds strange—how can greatness and exaltation be shown in death? John's answer seems to be that greatness is shown through free will. Jesus chose to die and through this great act he showed the fullness of love. Through the cross Jesus gained his kingship and life for all of us.

Free will is our gift from God, our ability to say "yes" or "no." Our world suffers; Jesus suffers and dies. Both events happen through free choice. Jesus' crucifixion shows us that free will, which has been used to cause so much pain, can lead to good; good can lead to love, and love can lead to salvation. Jesus' example of free will, his example of love, must be our path as well. We might not be able to change the system tomorrow, this year, or even in our lifetime. We can begin with ourselves, however, in following Jesus' law of love. Let us use our free will for good; let us use our free will for love. Let us use our free free will to sacrifice, to die for others, and in the process be exalted with Jesus to an eternal life with God.

Holy Saturday

Reflection on the Day

Waiting with God

"Something strange is happening—there is a great silence on earth today, a great silence and stillness. The whole earth keeps silence because the king is asleep. The earth trembled and is [now] still because the king is asleep. The earth trembled and is still because God has fallen asleep in the flesh and has raised up all who have slept ever since the world began. God has died in the flesh and hell trembles with fear."

So begins an ancient Patristic homily on Holy Saturday. A stillness has fallen on the earth. But something is not right; the quiet is not satisfying. The great events of yesterday somehow still leave us overwhelmed. How can God be dead? Jesus died in the flesh; but God is certainly not dead. No, Jesus is making preparations today for something truly glorious, something the world will never believe. How can one rise from the dead? We say it isn't possible, but forget that with God all things are possible.

The earth mourns, but not for long. The king is asleep, but the day of our salvation is at hand. If the world will not believe the resurrection from death of the Son of Man, will it believe in our own resurrection? We cannot even imagine what God is planning as he rests waiting for the great Easter morn. As St. Paul has put it so beautifully, "...no eye has seen, nor ear heard, nor the human heart conceived, what God has prepared for those who love him" (1 Cor 2:9).

In our preparation we have walked Lent's way of the cross; we have made ourselves ready to find God. Now we await the glory of the risen Christ to fill our lives with the brilliance which only God can give. Let us spend this day in calmness, but with great anticipation. As the early Christian homily says, God has raised up all who have fallen asleep. The promise of God, the gift of eternal life, will be ours as well.

Easter Sunday

Readings: Acts 10:34, 37-43;
Colossians 3:1-4; John 20:1-9

He Saw and Believed

"He saw and believed." These powerful words come from today's Gospel. What do they tell us about the Easter message? The words say and Easter reveals that we must find it in order to believe it.

In his novel *Siddhartha,* Hermann Hesse speaks of the search for life and meaning, telling a story of seeing and ultimately believing. Siddhartha was the son of a Brahman or holy man in the East. One day he went to his father and asked permission to leave the village of his birth to search for the meaning of life. Initially his father hesitated to let him go, but the boy insisted and so the older man allowed his son to leave. Siddhartha and his best friend gathered a few belongings and left the village the next day to search for the meaning of life.

As the boys began their journey they had traveled less than a day's walk from the village when they came upon a vast, wide river. Siddhartha looked upon the water and realized the emptiness which lay before him. He realized the meaning of life could not be found there; the river was vast but so empty. Their quest unfulfilled, the two boys hired a ferryman to take them to the other shore so they could continue their search.

After a few days of travel the boys came upon a group of ascetics, people who spend much time in prayer and reflection. Possibly, thought Siddhartha, the meaning of life could be found there. The boys asked permission from the community leader to join the group and learn the ways of prayer and meditation. The boys stayed for several years, growing into young adults. But after learning the ways of prayer and studying various methods of reflection, Siddhartha realized that the meaning of life was not to be found there either. Thus, the two friends moved on again.

After a few more days they came upon a guru or holy man. They attached themselves to those who followed this man. After a short while, however, Siddhartha knew that the meaning of life for him was not to be found there. His friend, however, found fulfillment, and thus, the two best friends parted company forever.

Siddhartha moved on in his quest to find the meaning of life and entered a great city. There he found work, love and marriage. He lived and worked in the city for many years and raised a family. Young adulthood turned to maturity and then to old age. Although he had spent most of his life in the great city, he still had not found the meaning of life.

Thus, as an old man, Siddhartha continued his search. He left the city and began to walk. The journey was long and tiring but he eventually came upon a river. It was the same river that he and his best friend had crossed so many years ago, when they had first left their home village. The river was still wide, vast and empty. But now Siddhartha looked at the river with new eyes.

He realized that he had spent his whole life trying to find the meaning of life by filling himself up. Now as an old man he came to the knowledge that the meaning of life had been before him, wherever he was, all along. He only needed to empty himself enough in order to see it.

What did John see and thus believe that day? He saw that the tomb was empty and realized that his life was full, cluttered with many things. The question for him was—could he empty himself enough to receive God, the risen Lord?

We need to ask ourselves the same question. Can we see and believe or are our lives too cluttered to receive God? We are all busy people, addicted to many things. Some of us are addicted to work; some are addicted to school. Some people are addicted to pleasure. Some, unfortunately, are addicted to themselves. At times we are so busy that our priorities get skewed. Sometimes our addictions come ahead of our God. It cannot be this way, if we are to see and believe!

We might not feel comfortable doing nothing, just being. It is difficult to accept the moment. However, if we empty ourselves somewhat then we can make room for God and his works. The reality of Jesus' resurrection is a message of hope for our own resurrection. But our resurrection need not wait until our union with God in eternity. We can begin now by emptying ourselves. If we are empty enough, if we are open, then we have chosen, as St. Paul suggests in today's second reading, the higher realm which comes from God. We will then be able to find God and in the process perform the works of the Lord, preaching, teaching, good works and healing.

Jesus' resurrection asks us to revive the human spirit deep inside each one of us. The empty tomb encourages us to be empty enough to be filled with God. Let us today rise to a new life; let us empty ourselves. Let us be refilled with the Lord, so that we too can see and believe!

Meditations for Special Feast Days of Lent

February 22—Chair of Peter

Readings: 1 Peter 5:1-4; Matthew 16:13-19

The Example of Love

People can learn in many ways. Through the educational system we spend a great deal of time learning through books and computers. Knowledge that others have gained is shared with us through the spoken and written word. We are a highly aural society these days. We listen to the radio, tapes and television. Much of what we know comes through our ability to hear.

The greatest way we can learn is through observation. Before children are old enough to read one word or understand a coherent sentence, they are learning. They learn by watching and imitation. Why do children possess so many common traits and habits of their parents? One reason certainly must be that they observe and do as they see. When we think about how people learn we recognize instantly the importance of example in our life. If we all learn by observation and example, then it is possible to learn both the right and the wrong ways of doing things. What we do and how we do it is very important, especially for those whom we most influence—family, friends and associates. People observe us whether we want it or not.

In celebrating the Chair of Peter we celebrate the office of the Pope. We celebrate the institution, but more importantly, as our readings suggest, we think of the responsibility that his office entails. The tradition of the Church has always held that Peter's profession of faith and subsequent commission by Jesus was the beginning of the office of the Papacy. Whether he knew it or chose it, Peter was given an awesome responsibility that day. He was to bind and to loose, but his responsibility was more fundamental. He must have eventually realized what it was, for he wrote about it in our first reading: "I exhort the elders among you to tend the flock of God that is in your charge, exercising the oversight, not under compulsion but willingly, as God would have you do it.... Be examples to the flock" (1 Pet 5:1-3).

The example that Peter was to give is our example as well. All who profess the name Christian are pastors in a certain sense. All of us have people for whom we are responsible. The responsibility may be with our family or in the community. Our principal responsibility may be at work. The example that we give to those people who look to us is critical, since people will do as they observe.

The example we give to others has specifics, but is best expressed in the way we live our life each day. We certainly will find many opportunities to show Christian behavior. This is our good example. More fundamentally, however, we must live our daily lives in such a way that others will want to do what we do. Our attitude is important in this regard. If we are joyful and positive about what we do then people will be attracted. It is equally true, however, that if we are glum and wear a frown in our daily lives, this too is powerfully communicated. We need to carry an attitude and example of love wherever we go. Then, the popular Christian hymn of past days will be fulfilled, "They'll know we are Christians by our love."

As we celebrate the Chair of Peter we remember the great responsibility held in the office of the Pope. Let us not forget our own responsibility, our own share in leading the flock. The Christian call is great; let us answer God's challenge this day with an example of love for all!

March 19—Feast of St. Joseph

Readings: 2 Samuel 7:4-5, 12-14, 16;
Romans 4:13, 16-18, 22;
Matthew 1:16, 18-21, 24 or Luke 2:41-51

The Faith of Parenthood

Unsettling statistics reveal a tragic situation for children in America. Each day the number of "unwanted" or rejected children rises. Some misplaced children are born out of wedlock while others are conceived through the violence of rape or incest. Although most people find it difficult to imagine, a growing number of children have been cast off by their biological parents almost as easily as a broken cup is tossed into a waste container. The disposable world has invaded the family and the results for society have been devastating. Children without the benefit of adult role models, especially those who lack a father, are more likely to lack good opportunities in life, such as education, and resort instead to lives of crime, violence and drugs. Violence in the home, including verbal, physical and sexual abuse of children, exacerbates an already grim situation. One wonders when people will come to their senses, take their responsibilities seriously, and carry out their duties as parents.

In celebrating the feast of St. Joseph, the foster father of Jesus, we are challenged to reflect upon the difficult but absolutely necessary task of being a good parent. Joseph serves as a model for all parents by the faith he exhibited so that God's plan of salvation for all people could come to fruition.

Joseph was asked to endure many things, some alone and others with his wife, Mary, all of which demanded great faith. In Matthew's Gospel we are told that God's messenger asked Joseph to take Mary as his wife despite the fact that she was pregnant. Moreover Joseph's faith was tested by the fact that his fiancée had conceived this child by the power of the Holy Spirit. In other words Joseph was asked by God to believe the impossible and take in a woman whom society would have shunned had the fact of her pregnancy been known.

Joseph was an upright man and a loving father, but his patience, along with Mary's, was tested when Jesus chose to stay behind in the Temple after the family's pilgrimage to Jerusalem for the Passover. He could not understand Jesus' needs, but he accepted in faith the fact that he could not comprehend all. God's plan would be completed and Joseph would do his part to build the kingdom on earth.

Joseph most certainly knew of his ancestral patriarch Abraham, and how God had asked him to demonstrate faith. God had promised Abraham that he would be the father of a great nation, but the fulfillment of God's word would take much time and Abraham would often be tested. Yet Abraham persevered, passed the test, and his faith was credited to him as righteousness.

Being a parent must be the most difficult task in today's hectic society. Parents face great demands, especially when both mother and father work outside the home. The myriad activities available to children and the unfortunate presence of many lurid temptations force parents to go beyond themselves to find solutions to many situations in which they find their children. It takes great faith to be a parent. Men and women must demonstrate faith in their ability to handle situations, in the wisdom and advice of people they trust, and in their children as well. All people, but especially parents, must place their faith in God, who desires that all humanity return home to him. God will never abandon any of us and will help us as we seek answers to problems which at times overwhelm us.

Parents have an awesome responsibility in today's world. Most parents are biological mothers and fathers, but others, like St. Joseph, serve an equally important role as foster parents. Faith is required for both; parenthood cannot be successfully managed without it. As we honor St. Joseph let us do our share to right the wrongs that have made children expendable while parents shrug off their responsibilities. Let us place our faith in ourselves, one another, our children, and God.

March 25—The Feast of the Annunciation

Readings: Isaiah 7:10-14;
Hebrews 10:4-10; Luke 1:26-38

Saying Yes to God's Plan

World history is replete with events which have defined the course of human society. William the Conqueror's invasion of England in 1066 had a tremendous impact on Great Britain. It linked England with France and paved the way for the eventual formation of the British Empire several centuries later. When Christopher Columbus landed on the island of San Salvador on October 12, 1492, the direction of the world took another major shift. Columbus' voyage set in motion a whole series of events affecting Europe and the New World. Adolph Hitler's order of a blitzkrieg attack on Poland on September 1, 1939, plunged the world into a war which produced the greatest human carnage in history. The war wiped out millions of people, shifted the map, and was the catalyst behind the development of the nuclear weapons which shroud the world with fear.

Organized religion has also experienced several events which have defined its course in history. The conversion of Emperor Constantine in 313 to Christianity gave the Church legal status, allowed it to spread, and changed the course of Western civilization. On October 31, 1517, Martin Luther nailed his famous "Ninety-Five Theses" to the door of the castle church in Wittenberg.

This act sparked the Reformation and the division of the Church, a situation which continues to this day. For Catholics, in the opinion of the famous 20th century German Jesuit Karl Rahner, the start of the Second Vatican Council on October 11, 1962, began a new era in the direction and history of the Church.

Most events which have defined the direction of the world, both its secular and religious paths, are well-known by date and place. We read about these events in our history books and are required to know them for examinations. The most important defining moment in all human history, the event which climaxed God's plan for the salvation of all people, the Annunciation, cannot be so accurately situated in historical context. We know that it took place but precisely when and where was never recorded. Yet, this event which is celebrated today helped bring to fulfillment God's plan of salvation history.

The Annunciation had been predicted but it went unnoticed by the world. The prophet Isaiah wrote, "Therefore the Lord himself will give you a sign. Look, the young woman is with child and shall bear a son, and shall name him Immanuel" (7:14). The day of the Annunciation, like most "defining" events, was not so understood when it occurred; its importance was seen only after the great events of Jesus' life and his passion, death, and resurrection. The Annunciation is celebrated in our churches, but its relevance in leading the world to salvation has transformed the world and channeled all our lives in a direction which enables our actions and words to build God's kingdom on earth. The Annunciation as an event gave us a reason and purpose for life.

The celebration of this great event today challenges us to understand Mary's great *fiat,* her "yes" to God and our need to imitate her courage. Human beings have been endowed by God with all sorts of wonderful gifts which we use in our daily lives to build the kingdom. In many ways, the gifts we possess define who we are. If we have been given the gift of words we will probably be known as a writer, orator or preacher. The ability to teach and convey knowledge to others will place us in the classroom. Skill with our hands also defines us as a carpenter, mechanic or artist. Athletes find fulfillment on the baseball diamond, the gridiron or the basketball court. The gifts we possess define in many ways who we are and often dictate the path in life we will follow.

One gift, however, is common to all and defines us as human—the gift of free will. No one has more or less free will; it is a special, but general and equal gift of God. Its very nature means that how we use our free will is up to us. It can be used to do good and benefit society or, if used with evil intent, can cast us into darkness. Mary said "yes" when the angel Gabriel brought God's invitation that special day. She had free choice and decided as the author of the Letter to the Hebrews suggests, "I have come to do your will" (10:7). Mary had no special insight into the future when she consented. Like all young people she had dreams and hopes and she knew that this decision would change all her plans. But Mary used the gift which defined her humanity to bring the possibility of salvation to all people for all time. She did not understand this but she did possess great faith: "Now faith is the assurance of things hoped for, the conviction of things not seen" (Heb 11:1).

ALASKA
750 West 5th Ave., Anchorage, AK 99501; 907-272-8183

CALIFORNIA
3908 Sepulveda Blvd., Culver City, CA 90230; 310-397-8676
5945 Balboa Ave., San Diego, CA 92111; 619-565-9181
46 Geary Street, San Francisco, CA 94108; 415-781-5180

FLORIDA
145 S.W. 107th Ave., Miami, FL 33174; 305-559-6715

HAWAII
1143 Bishop Street, Honolulu, HI 96813; 808-521-2731

ILLINOIS
172 North Michigan Ave., Chicago, IL 60601; 312-346-4228

LOUISIANA
4403 Veterans Memorial Blvd., Metairie, LA 70006; 504-887-7631

MASSACHUSETTS
50 St. Paul's Ave., Jamaica Plain, Boston, MA 02130; 617-522-8911
Rte. 1, 885 Providence Hwy., Dedham, MA 02026; 617-326-5385

MISSOURI
9804 Watson Rd., St. Louis, MO 63126; 314-965-3512

NEW JERSEY
561 U.S. Route 1, Wick Plaza, Edison, NJ 08817; 908-572-1200

NEW YORK
150 East 52nd Street, New York, NY 10022; 212-754-1110
78 Fort Place, Staten Island, NY 10301; 718-447-5071

OHIO
2105 Ontario Street, Cleveland, OH 44115; 216-621-9427

PENNSYLVANIA
9171-A Roosevelt Blvd., Philadelphia, PA
19114; 215-676-9494

SOUTH CAROLINA
243 King Street, Charleston, SC 29401; 803-577-0175

TENNESSEE
4811 Poplar Ave., Memphis, TN 38117; 901-761-2987

TEXAS
114 Main Plaza, San Antonio, TX 78205; 210-224-8101

VIRGINIA
1025 King Street, Alexandria, VA 22314; 703-549-3806

CANADA
3022 Dufferin Street, Toronto, Ontario, Canada M6B 3T5; 416-781-9131
1155 Yonge Street, Toronto, Ontario, Canada M4T 1W2; 416-934-3440